B R E A K
A W A Y
A M I S H

"*Breakaway Amish* is an honest, insightful, insider's view of the strange doings among the Bergholz beard cutters, whose troubles intrigued and appalled the nation. Seldom do outsiders get such a revealing glimpse of what happens to an isolated group when, as Johnny Mast writes, 'You learn to ignore the voices in your head telling you, This isn't right. None of this is right.' An eyewitness account of a leader's twisted descent into mental hell and of the havoc it can cause among people who only seek to be devout and faithful."

—TOM SHACHTMAN, AUTHOR OF *RUMSPRINGA: TO BE OR NOT TO BE AMISH*

"Absolutely riveting! What an honest account of how the Bergholz community starts out 'nice and Amish' and then goes down a dark road. Thank goodness Johnny Mast had the courage to break away, find his rightful path, and write this book!"

—SALOMA MILLER FURLONG, AUTHOR OF *WHY I LEFT THE AMISH* AND *BONNET STRINGS*

"*Breakaway Amish* is a riveting story of betrayal. Johnny Mast should have been able to count on the love and faith of his family. Instead he was manipulated by his grandfather, Sam Mullet, who turned his pacifist Amish community into an aggressive, revenge-seeking cult. In this heartbreaking eyewitness account of life in the Bergholz community, Mast recounts the slow descent of his family and friends into isolation, violence, and physical and sexual abuse. Sadly, for telling the truth, Johnny Mast has been ostracized by the very people who should have protected him."

—KAREN JOHNSON-WEINER, COAUTHOR OF *THE AMISH*

"A normal Amish youth, Johnny Mast grows up into the ways of his fathers, with the simple hopes and dreams common in such a world. But then comes a dark turn down bleak roads, not only for Johnny but for an entire community caught in the grip of bishop Sam Mullet's powerful and destructive personality. This raw, riveting insider's account of a strange and chilling story is absolutely unique in the annals of Amish history."

—IRA WAGLER, AUTHOR OF *GROWING UP AMISH*

BREAK AWAY AMISH

GROWING UP

with the

BERGHOLZ

BEARD

CUTTERS

JOHNNY MAST

with SHAWN SMUCKER

Foreword by DONALD B. KRAYBILL

Herald Press

Harrisonburg, Virginia
Kitchener, Ontario

Library of Congress Cataloging-in-Publication Data
Names: Mast, Johnny, 1990- author. | Smucker, Shawn, author.
Title: Breakaway Amish : growing up with the Bergholz beard cutters / Johnny
    Mast with Shawn Smucker.
Description: Harrisonburg, Virginia : Herald Press, [2016]
Identifiers: LCCN 2016008106 (print) | LCCN 2016015246 (ebook) | ISBN
    9781513800219 (pbk. : alk. paper) | ISBN 9781513801049 (hardcover : alk.
    paper) | ISBN 9781513800226 (ebook)
Subjects: LCSH: Mast, Johnny, 1990- | Hate crimes--Ohio--Amish Country. |
    Amish--Violence against--Ohio--Amish Country. | Amish--Ohio. |
    Amish--Customs and practices. | Amish--Doctrines. | Violence--Religious
    aspects--Amish. | Beards--Religious aspects. | Hair--Religious aspects.
Classification: LCC HV6773.53.O3 M37 2016 (print) | LCC HV6773.53.O3
    (ebook)
    | DDC 364.15/55--dc23
LC record available at https://lccn.loc.gov/2016008106

This is a work of nonfiction and as such, the author has attempted to adhere to the facts of the events described. Every effort has been made to ensure that the events occurred as the author has described.

BREAKAWAY AMISH
© 2016 by Herald Press, Harrisonburg, Virginia 22802
    Released simultaneously in Canada by Herald Press,
    Kitchener, Ontario N2G 3R1. All rights reserved.
Library of Congress Control Number: 2016008106
International Standard Book Number: 978-1-5138-0021-9 (paperback edition)
International Standard Book Number: 978-1-5138-0104-9 (hardcover edition)
Printed in United States of America
Cover and interior design by Reuben Graham
Photo on p. 118 courtesy of Willard/iStock/Thinkstock. Unless attributed otherwise, other interior photos are courtesy of the author or used as evidence in the trial.

For orders or information, call 800-245-7894 or visit HeraldPress.com.

20 19 18 17 16   11 10 9 8 7 6 5 4 3 2

CONTENTS

FOREWORD

Breakaway Amish is not only about growing up in a wayward Amish group. Johnny Mast's story, which he and Shawn Smucker tell so ably in these pages, is a story of human tragedy. It chronicles what happens when men, in the name of God, abuse positions of power to exploit, harm, and denigrate others. It's an important, cautionary tale, and the rest of us would do well to listen carefully.

I first learned to know Johnny Mast when I read his lengthy testimony at the three-week federal trial in Cleveland in 2012. We both testified at the trial but never met each other. As a witness for the prosecution, he provided a riveting account that incriminated his grandfather, bishop Sam Mullet, and fifteen other members of a breakaway Amish community in eastern Ohio. Among other crimes, the sixteen defendants were found guilty of federal hate crimes for attacking Amish people in several different counties.

Johnny and a couple of his teenage cousins lived in a second-floor apartment of their grandfather's barn. Johnny, whom his grandfather favored, had the inside scoop on everything leading up to the attacks. He was an eyewitness to the FBI's surprise arrests in the early morning darkness just before Thanksgiving 2011.

All the Bergholz defendants were sentenced to federal prisons. The court gave Johnny's grandfather, the ringleader of the church, a fifteen-year term. A journalist who later visited Bergholz told me that Johnny wanted a copy of my book *Renegade Amish: Beard Cutting, Hate Crimes, and the Trial of the Bergholz Barbers*. I sent him a copy, and we talked occasionally by telephone and email. I learned that he and some of his cousins had left Bergholz and were living on their own for the first time. I was so impressed with Johnny's grasp of the Bergholz tragedy, his levelheadedness and mature self-understanding, that on a whim I invited him to a one-day seminar—"Hate Crimes and the Bergholz Barbers"—organized by the Young Center for Anabaptist and Pietist Studies at Elizabethtown (Pa.) College.

Early on the morning of that conference, I met Johnny for the first time over sausage and pancakes in the breakfast bar of a hotel. I was anxious. I had no idea if inviting him was a wise or foolish move. I knew this was the first time he would step on a college campus. He had never addressed a public audience about Bergholz. But I soon relaxed. At the conference, Johnny spoke and answered questions for about an hour. He was calm, clear, and thoughtful, and he didn't appear embittered by his Bergholz trauma.

After the seminar, we met privately for about two hours before he returned to Ohio. He wanted to write a book. "Why?" I asked. Because, he said, so much gossip, innuendo, and false information continued to swirl around about the Bergholz events. Nobody knew the truth. Nobody, he said, had ever told the truth from an insider's perspective. He worried that the same excruciating tragedy could visit other Amish churches—or churches of any kind. Johnny worried that leaders in other churches might become authoritarian, deceitful, and abusive, threatening people and leading them astray. I was struck by his sincerity, integrity, and passion for truth telling.

I gladly explained to him some dos and don'ts about writing and publishing. I offered to meet him again and accompany him to meet with a publisher. Several months later, in Geauga County, Ohio, about eight miles from where his grandfather grew up, I met with Johnny, his girlfriend, Clara, and a publisher to talk more about a book.

I'm grateful that Johnny had the courage and conviction to tell the truth in the pages that follow. No one has ever done this before. It was not easy for him. It's not a pleasant story with a happy ending. But it is an important story, and a hard book to put down.

—*Donald B. Kraybill, author of* Renegade Amish

I've described all the events to the best of my recollection. Situations and conversations may be composites of my experience and imagination given that precise statements are not easily recalled. The dialogue included is meant to convey the tone of the conversations and does not reflect word-for-word conversations that took place (except in the case of courtroom dialogue, which has been taken directly from court transcripts).

If I've missed any crucial details or retold anything out of order, I apologize.

—*Johnny Mast*

Sam Mullet, the bishop of Bergholz and my grandfather. Associated Press Photo / Amy Sancetta.

PART I
When Bergholz Changed

1

WITNESS FOR THE PROSECUTION

I stared at the courtroom door in front of me and took a deep breath, trying to figure out how things had gotten to this point. I was only an Amish kid working construction and selling horses on the side. I didn't know anything about trials or courtrooms or hate crimes. I didn't know anything about perjury or federal statutes or juries. I definitely didn't know anything about being a witness for the prosecution.

But on that day, that's exactly what I was.

I walked into the courtroom. I wondered when I'd be asked about the camera. I wondered how much the lawyers had heard about Sam and his relationships with the women in our community. I heard a few whispers as I walked down the aisle, and then everyone grew silent as I took the stand.

I had been called there to testify against my grandfather, Samuel Mullet, as well as the other men and women in our Amish community who had been involved in the things that had happened during the previous year.

My knees felt like jelly. The bailiff swore me in. I was glad to sit down, even if it was in the witness stand. The judge was to my left, and he spoke first. He was matter-of-fact and firm.

"All right. I'm advising you that your testimony is being compelled, pursuant to federal statute Title 18. Sections 600(2) and 600(3), and that as a result, no testimony that you give in response to questions can be used against you in any future criminal proceeding."

He paused and shuffled through some papers in front of him.

"However, should you testify falsely in any manner, the statements could be used and you could be prosecuted for perjury. Do you understand this?"

I tried to keep my voice even, but it had a life of its own.

"Yes," I said.

"All right," the judge stated. "Do you have any questions about this, sir?"

"No," I said.

"Okay. Thank you," the judge said.

Both the prosecution and the defense wanted to use me for their own purposes, and I had met with them in the months and weeks leading up to the trial. "Don't say more than you have to," Sam's attorney had stressed to me during pretrial meetings. "If you can answer with only a yes or no, do it. Try to get the attorney to phrase the question so you can answer simply yes or no. Otherwise, just say 'I don't know.'"

The prosecuting attorney stood up and walked around to the front of her table. My grandmother (Sam's wife) and all the spouses of the defendants sat in chairs on the left side of the courtroom. Amish people from other communities sat on the right. There were reporters and a lot of people I didn't know. The room was full and quiet. I wasn't sure where to look. I cleared my throat and took a deep breath.

"Good morning," the attorney said to me. "Please state your name and spell your last name for the record."

"Johnny Mast," I said. "M-A-S-T."

"Mr. Mast, where do you live?"

"Bergholz, Ohio."

When I said the name of our town out loud, I thought about all the things that had been written about us in the newspapers. *The Bergholz Beard Cutters.*

All sixteen defendants, including my grandfather, sat at different tables in front of me, a little to the left. I'm sure they were nervous about what I would say and how my words would affect them. Some of them faced years and years in prison. The men's hair was flat against their heads from the hats they wore that morning on the way to the courthouse. They stared blankly at the table or the wall at first, but at the sound of my voice they looked up at me.

"And where specifically in Bergholz, Ohio, do you live?"

"I'm at my parents' place."

"Are you related to defendant Sam Mullet, Senior?"

"Yes."

"And how is that?"

I took a deep breath.

"He's my grandfather."

I glanced over at Sam and he returned my gaze with a mischievous sparkle in his eyes. He grinned and nodded. He had been nothing but supportive to me in the days leading up to my testimony, even though I was supposed to testify against him. He encouraged me to tell the truth and to remember the advice his lawyer gave me. I couldn't help but give a small smile back before looking away. I knew I probably shouldn't look at him. I couldn't believe I had to testify against him. He had done a lot of strange things, a lot of things I didn't understand. But he was still my grandfather.

"And so Samuel Mullet's sons are your uncles?"

"Yes."

"And defendant Linda Shrock is your aunt?"

"Yes."

I settled into the game of questions and answers. Questions and answers, and every so often objections by the other attorneys. Yes and no and I don't know and more objections.

"How old are you, Mr. Mast?"

"Twenty-two."

"Have you been baptized into the Amish church in Bergholz?"

"Yes."

"Was there a time when members of the Bergholz community cut each other's hair and beards?"

I paused. I saw images in my mind that made me wince. Images I'd rather forget: Holding my own father's hair in my hands and cutting off pieces with a pair of scissors. Watching six or seven men wander down toward Sam's barn, chunks of their hair shaved off, their beards cut straight across with sharp scissors. I remember seeing those disheveled men, skinny from not having eaten, their weird hair and their hats that no longer fit quite right, and thinking they looked like demons.

"Yes."

"When did that first start happening?"

"Probably about three years ago."

"And what was your understanding of what the reason for it was?"

"Because they weren't living their life the way they knew they should, and they wanted to turn their life around."

It made me nervous when I gave long answers. I was scared of the words coming out of my mouth, scared that they would somehow implicate Sam or the others.

"So it was a symbol of a new start?"

"Yes."

"Did you ever have your hair or beard cut during this time?"

"No."

"Were you present when others had their hair or beards cut?"

"Yes."

Again I pictured my own father, and I heard Sam's voice. *C'mon, Johnny, cut off some of your dad's hair. You're mad at him too, aren't you?*

The attorney kept firing questions at me. I concentrated, tried hard to keep my answers short.

"Was Sam Mullet, Senior, aware of the practice of beard cutting within the community?"

"Yes."

"And did some of the beard cuttings actually take place in his presence?"

"Yes."

"What was your understanding of what Sam Mullet, Senior, thought of these beard cuttings in terms of their ability to help people turn their lives around?"

Sam's defense lawyer called out, and it startled me.

"Objection!"

"Sustained," said the judge, nodding.

The prosecution paused, then asked the question in a different way.

"Did you ever discuss these beard cuttings with Sam Mullet, Senior?"

"Could you ask that question again?" I asked.

"Yes. Did you ever discuss the use of beard and hair cuttings within the community with Sam Mullet, Senior?"

"Yes."

"And what did he say about the use of beard and hair cuttings when you discussed it with him?"

"He didn't know if it would be the right thing to do or not. He wasn't sure."

The attorney turned around and looked at papers on her desk, then turned toward me again.

"Did there come a time you heard members of the Bergholz community talking about cutting the head and beard hair of Amish people who lived outside of the community?"

I paused. This was exactly why we were all there. I remembered the Millers, the Hershbergers, the Shrocks. I remembered being handed a trash bag full of hair and being told to burn it out back. I remembered the sound of shouts. I remembered the sound of a man's roar, a man who was trying to defend himself.

"Yes," I said.

2

THE MOVE TO BERGHOLZ

I fell in love with horses long before we moved to Bergholz, back when I was only five or six years old and my dad took me to the Mount Hope horse auction. He was in the market for a team of workhorses, and I was excited when he asked me to go along. We got there and I looked around in awe. There were horses everywhere, some moving and restless, others standing still as statues. They were different colors, different temperaments, and I wanted to pet them all. There, at my first horse auction, I was filled with this desire to own horses, and lots of them.

Dad bought two workhorses on that particular morning: nice ones. Our driver hauled them home for us. The Amish travel mostly by horse and buggy, but if they need to go somewhere too far for that, they hire a non-Amish person to drive them around. It's a common thing, and some drivers make a full-time living just driving Amish folks from here to there.

I remember the first time we hooked the horses to the big old box wagon before heading out to the woods to get firewood. I was standing in the box, and Dad let me drive our new horses. I felt like a million dollars, even though the horses were tame and probably could have done it on their own. When I felt the horses' energy come through the reins, I knew I was a horse man.

I know everyone says tractors are better, and of course I agree that they're faster. But I always found something peaceful about being up there behind the horses, the sound of the wagon creaking through the field, the horses' tails swishing away the flies. It's quiet when you're out in a field driving horses. It feels like there's nothing else in the world.

Not too long after my dad bought those workhorses, I got my first pony. We bought it from my uncle. When my dad brought it out of the trailer, my brother Floyd held it by the lead rope. The pony came out and stood there quietly, eating grass. But it must have stepped over the lead rope, because when my brother pulled the rope taut, it tightened up under the pony and startled it. That crazy pony—it ran off and got away from us. We couldn't catch it. We ended up chasing it all over the neighborhood, through fields and people's yards. It was taller than me and ornery as anything. I was scared half to death of that sucker, and even though I was chasing it, I secretly hoped my brother would be the one to catch it.

I've always felt a connection between me and my dad and my horses, probably ever since he took me to that horse auction when I was little. I miss having horses. I miss Bergholz the way it was when we first arrived.

It would be nice to see my dad again, to be able to have a regular conversation. But what happened in Bergholz ruined all of that.

I was eleven years old when we moved to Bergholz, Ohio. We had been living in a community about 120 miles west of there, but I wasn't sad to be leaving that place. I don't think any of us in the family were. It never felt as if that first community accepted our family. For some reason I felt that we were looked down on, pushed out to the side, and I didn't have any close friends there. Sometimes I'd play with other boys, but as soon as someone else showed up, I was alone again.

When we moved to Bergholz, everything changed for me.

The town of Bergholz still looks almost the same as it did the first time we approached it in a moving truck, driving on those back country roads. I liked the mountains, the way the land rose and fell with lots of hills and valleys. There are more houses now than there were when we moved there, mostly because of all the gas wells going in. But even now there are roads in Bergholz that will take you to places way back in, miles from any other houses.

My grandfather, Sam Mullet, had started the Bergholz Amish community six or seven years before we moved there. He and my grandmother bought a farm about three miles outside of town, and a few families—mostly his children, my aunts and uncles, and their families—followed them. There's a little old dirt road that goes back to his place, lined for a little ways with a wooden fence that my brother Edward and I built.

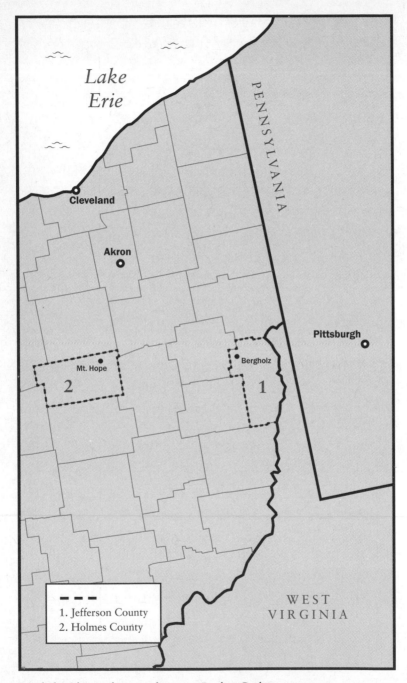

Bergholz, Ohio, and surrounding area. Reuben Graham.

The community started their own church, as Amish communities do when they start up in a new area, and Sam became our bishop. It made sense at the time. Who else would lead the new community? Most of the men there were Sam's sons or sons-in-law. Sam had bought the first piece of land. The whole community had been Sam's idea.

Bergholz was a whole new world for me. I was suddenly surrounded by tons of cousins who became my best friends. I attended our Amish school with thirty or thirty-five other students, and we had a lot of fun. Because Sam, my own grandfather, was the bishop of the church, I felt I really belonged there. All the community events, like picnics or holiday meals, took place at his house. We were a tight group.

More and more families arrived every year, drawn by the fact that we were practicing a strict version of the Amish lifestyle. We didn't have indoor plumbing. No one had a phone except Sam. No cars, no tractors, and no radios or televisions. No cell phones. You'd be amazed at how many people want to live a simple life, removed from the chaos and the busyness of the outside world. It was a thriving community.

There weren't any physical fences or gates that defined the edges of the community. People asked about that, after everything came out. I think people expected it to look like a compound, but it wasn't that way at all. Our Bergholz community was open, without any gates or walls to define it. There might have been ten miles between the two families that lived farthest from each other.

So there weren't any boundaries—not physical ones, anyway. But I've been back a few times since, and it's almost as if I can feel the trees closing in around me. Sam somehow managed to create the feeling of walls all around us. Invisible walls. Walls we would never be able to cross over, or get through. I guess that's why some people are still there. Those invisible walls.

"I see one," my dad said.

I stopped, frozen in place, and searched the forest floor. We had left our home, walked through some fields to a stream, and then crossed the stream by walking on a beaver dam. Leaving the dairy farm behind us, we searched through the beaver dam until we found a good walking stick. I kept some of the really good ones back at the house, but as the years passed, they all got misplaced. I wish I still had one of those walking sticks.

We entered the forest on the other side of the stream and hiked up the hill. We often took walks together up into those woods, especially on Sunday afternoons. Sometimes my brothers came along, and sometimes it was just me and my dad. Sundays that we didn't have church were the best time for Dad and me to walk up into the forest and look for mushrooms.

At the top of the hill was a remote field that was difficult to find. If you didn't cross by the beaver dam, you had to walk a mile or more out around and make your way through briars and woods. A guy had an old school bus set up there. It was broken down and didn't run, but he had fixed up the inside so he could use it as a camper. We'd go up there and my brothers and I would play around the bus for a little while, and then we'd head home.

Anyway, to be honest, I was never any good at finding mushrooms. I would walk all over them without even realizing it. But Dad could spot anything. He would point out deer tracks in the soft ground, and we would make plans for where we'd hunt in the fall.

My dad pointed at the ground. I tried to see what he was seeing. "There's another mushroom," he said. "Do you see it?"

"Really?" I asked him, still looking. "You see one?"

"Oh, there's another one," he said.

"Dad!"

He laughed. Then I saw it: a small mushroom creeping up through the leaves.

"There it is!" I said, laughing, running over to grab it. We shuffled the leaves around and found an entire patch of

My parents' farm in Bergholz.

mushrooms, hidden there in the dark soil. We picked them and headed back to the house, walking slowly, the Sunday evening light fading behind the trees.

I turned twelve years old soon after we moved to Bergholz, which meant I didn't have to sit with Dad in church anymore. I could finally sit with the other boys my own age. I was pretty excited to get to church that day.

We had a long drive that morning, so we had hooked up two horses to the seated buggy. I was starting to feel a little nervous about sitting in church without my dad. I helped him unhook the horses, and they were sweaty from the long ride. Just as I went to put one of the tugs up, the horse started slapping at a fly with its tail. Wouldn't you know, that old horse hit me right in the face with its nasty, stinky, sweaty tail. It was disgusting.

I had to go behind the barn and try to wash all that off before heading in for church. We went inside the house where church was being held that week. I sat with my friends, and it felt good. I didn't feel like a little kid anymore.

The peace we felt there in Bergholz lasted about five years. Those years came one after the other, and they passed quickly. I knew it would soon be time for me to think about joining the church. It's a big decision, you know, when an Amish teenager decides to join the church. It's a decision for life.

It was about that time when things started falling apart.

3

WHEN THE DEVIL CAME TO BERGHOLZ

I don't know too much about the early problems that took place in Bergholz, because those happened just before I joined the church. I was still hanging out with the young people. We did our own thing and weren't involved in official Bergholz business. It was my parents who went to all the meetings, my parents and their friends who stayed up talking late into the night. I could hear their voices in the kitchen as I fell asleep, but I couldn't hear what they were saying.

But I do remember two things that happened.

The first took place after church one Sunday. I was outside with some of my friends, relieved that church was over. Services are long and slow and quiet. The preacher speaks in German, which is kind of hard to understand. We had just been set free for the afternoon.

On that particular Sunday, I was out there with my friends when I saw a few families leave the house where church had been held. But instead of joining everyone else for lunch, they hitched up their buggies and drove away. I stood there watching the dust cloud rise up behind them, and an uneasy feeling filled me. It was strange for families to leave straight after church. I was old enough to know that if someone didn't stay for lunch, they were being disciplined by the church leadership, which was my grandfather Sam. I knew something was going on, but I didn't ask about it.

During the next few months, there was a lot of whispering, a lot of rumors. A few folks sided with the Troyers, one of the families who didn't agree with some of the things Sam was saying and doing. Most sided with Sam. He was the bishop, after all, the leader of our community. And he wasn't the sort of person you wanted to side against. He had a way of making your life miserable if you did.

Soon Sam forced the families that sided with the Troyers to sit in a separate room during church. I think they had been told to stay there until they agreed with Sam. That's when families started leaving. The Troyers were the first to go, followed by the Yoders and the Shrocks.

I'd say it was within the next six to twelve months when a large group of ministers first talked about what they should do about Bergholz. They appointed a committee to figure out what was going on in our community. That was in June 2006. Then a few months later, in September, a few hundred Amish bishops from all over Ohio and Pennsylvania and West Virginia met together to talk about what Sam was doing at Bergholz and whether the families leaving Bergholz could join other Amish communities. They called it "the problem of Bergholz." You see, normally if you leave an Amish community while under church discipline, you can't join another community until you make things right with the community you left. But some of the people leaving

Bergholz complained that when Sam heard you were leaving, he'd put you under church discipline just to try and keep you in Bergholz. That way you couldn't leave and join another community.

This huge group of Amish bishops met, and that kind of meeting is rare among the Amish. I had never heard of one like it before. These bishops eventually made a decision that went against Sam's leadership. That is, the families who left Bergholz would be allowed to join other Amish communities without bowing down to Sam's wishes. It basically meant they didn't consider his shunning legitimate.

Sam was irate.

Someone within Bergholz made an observation about the June meeting of Amish leaders, an observation that seemed to make us Bergholz folks feel better. I don't know if it was Sam or his son Johnny Mullet or someone else who pointed it out, but they said to take note that the Amish bishops met on June 6, 2006.

6/6/06.

666.

For us, it became a sign that the gathering of Amish bishops had been a meeting of evil people. They were on the side of the devil, and we were on the right side, the side of God. At least that's the rumor that started circulating around Bergholz. It wasn't long before Sam started spinning everything as good against evil, us against them.

It wasn't long after that when, in his words, "the devil came to Bergholz."

One Sunday we had church at my uncle Eli Mullet's house. I was old enough to know that things were getting worse in our community. Something was going on, something that wasn't good. More families had left, and those who remained behind started to separate into small groups. It just didn't feel right.

On that particular Sunday, my uncle Eli Mullet wasn't himself. He had been acting strangely all day, talking loudly to himself and walking around the outskirts of where we were all sitting. After church we usually had lunch together, but he just wandered around, not talking to anyone in particular.

My mother told me that later that night, after almost everyone had left, Eli sat around with my grandfather Sam and my grandmother Martha. Eli leaned in and asked them a serious question.

"If it came to the point where you had to admit that you were wrong and the Troyers were right, could you do it?" The Troyers had been one of the first families to stand up to Sam.

Sam stared at Eli and waited before answering.

"No, I wouldn't do it."

Eli turned his gaze to his mother, Martha. She seemed a little less certain.

"Would you admit you were wrong?" he asked.

"I don't know," she said. "Probably not."

The next day Eli Mullet went to the town of Rogers and worked with an old guy who trained horses. Rogers is about thirty miles away, and Eli helped there with the horseshoeing and horse training. Well, that night Eli didn't get home, not until early Tuesday morning. Sam went over there that night to talk to Eli and see what was wrong, why he had been acting so strange lately, and why he hadn't gotten home until so late.

When Sam arrived, Eli was all out of sorts. Eli's wife tried to explain it away, but Sam had his own opinion about what was wrong with Eli.

Sam said, matter-of-factly, that it must be the devil.

It's the devil. What did Sam mean?

Concern for Eli spread through the community. People began to wonder what was going on with Eli. Was he mentally unstable or, as Sam suggested, was he possessed by the devil? On Wednesday night of that week, my parents went down to Sam's house to see how everything was going. After all, Eli was my mom's brother, and I think she was worried for him. My oldest brother went along, so it was up to me to watch the rest of the kids, including my two-year-old sister.

The night stretched on, and no matter what I did, I couldn't get my little sister to go to sleep. My other siblings drifted off, but she kept crying. I started to feel overwhelmed, and I wondered when my parents would get home. I woke up one of the kids and sent them over to Jonas Yoder's house for help. Turns out the Yoders weren't home either—they had gone to Sam's house too. But my brother's girlfriend was home, so she came over and took care of the baby while I got some sleep.

She watched my sister from around eleven until two in the morning, but soon she came and knocked on my door.

"I just can't get her to quiet down," she said, yawning. "Do you mind taking another turn?"

So we went back and forth like that all night, and neither one of us got much sleep. All this time I wondered where my parents were and what could have gone so wrong that they were kept away all night.

Later I found out what had been going on.

Eli Mullet was losing his mind, or at least that's how it looked. He would run off into the woods, and people could hear him shouting from far away. Then he'd come racing back to where everyone had gathered.

"Do you see Eli?" he asked each of them, his eyes wild. "Or do you see the devil?"

He ran into the woods again and some time later came back.

"Don't wait too long!" Eli shouted like an Old Testament prophet. "God doesn't wait! It's the devil trying to make you wait! Don't wait! You have to repent now! You have to do good things now! You have to forgive people now!"

Eventually my uncles Danny Mullet, Johnny Mullet, and Eli Hostetler held Eli to the ground to keep him from running off. They held him there all night and didn't let him get up, not even for a coat or a blanket. I guess they were worried about what he might do, or what they seemed to think the devil might do through him.

I didn't know it at the time, but there were already shameful things going on in the community, and Eli knew about them. He had seen strange things going on, things that shouldn't happen in any community, much less an Amish one. I guess that's what he was talking about—the people involved in those things needed to repent, and they needed to do it now. But I didn't know about any of the bad stuff, so I didn't have any idea what Eli was talking about. He just sounded as though he was losing his mind.

Eli's behavior scared everyone, and his prophetic decrees had an effect on my dad, who vowed off tobacco products that night. In Bergholz, tobacco was off-limits: no smoking, no chewing, nothing. My dad had chewed tobacco since he was sixteen years old, basically his entire life, so he had snuck around Bergholz hiding his habit. He had tried to wean himself off it, but he always went back for more.

That night, though, after seeing Eli, my dad had enough. That was it. He was done. There was something about that strange experience that unsettled my dad. When he and mom got back that morning, around five thirty, he got all his tobacco and threw it in the stove. I know, because I was standing there with my brother's girlfriend and my baby sister when they got home.

We had hardly slept all night, and they hadn't at all.

Eli was becoming something of a nightly attraction, especially in a community like ours where this sort of thing was unheard of. Most non-Amish people might have at least seen someone having a mental breakdown like this on television or in the movies. But for us it was a first, and it was real life. So later that day, everyone in the community starting showing up at Sam's to find out how Eli was doing.

Soon someone realized Eli was standing in the driveway, so everyone gathered in the yard beside him. We didn't know what to do.

"Larry?" he shouted in a shaky voice. "Where's Larry?"

I assumed he was talking about Larry, the guy he worked with up in Rogers.

"Where are all my friends?" he shouted. No one said anything.

He stopped talking for a moment. Everything was silent. No one moved.

"I hear a horse. I hear a horse. Yeah, Larry. I hear a horse."

I looked around, feeling as though someone needed to do something, say something. I heard someone using a chainsaw off in the distance.

"A chainsaw! I hear a chainsaw!" Eli shouted. "I hear a horse!"

A strange sense of doom settled around us. What was going on? Was this something spiritual? Was the devil in our midst?

"If you hear Eli talking, sit down, but if you think this is the devil talking, stay standing," Eli demanded.

Everyone stood there, frozen. He repeated himself, louder this time.

"I said, if you hear Eli talking, then sit down. But if you hear the devil talking, stay standing!"

Everyone sat down in the grass. All around us the fields and the trees were silent. As soon as everyone sat down, he put his hands straight up above his head and fell flat on his back. It was one of the craziest things I've ever seen.

He suddenly scrambled to his feet, looked around like a hunted animal, and sprinted past Sam's house and into the woods. We could hear him yelling, and his voice trailed off as he vanished into the trees.

"I hear a horse!"

"I hear a chainsaw!"

"Where's Larry?"

A few days later, Eli went missing.

It was in the afternoon, and we all gathered at Sam's house before heading out to the woods and the fields to look for him. I heard the other people calling out. "Eli!" "Eli!" "Eli!"

No one could find him, and we started getting nervous. I guess we all had our fears about what might have happened to Eli, but no one really talked about it.

It turns out he had hiked out to the main road and flagged down a coal truck. The driver stopped and Eli jumped onto the side of it, jabbering away as the guy drove down the road. He rode this way on a few different coal trucks. Finally, one of the truck drivers brought him back to Bergholz.

"You need to do something about this man," the driver said before he left. "He's crazy. He's out in the middle of the road, stopping trucks. You have to do something. You can't just let someone like this roam the countryside."

Later that night Sam and my uncle Johnny Mullet were sitting in Sam's house when Eli came in and starting getting loud. I don't know exactly what happened, but I think it involved a gun.

Sam finally decided to call the cops. Several police officers came out to Bergholz, but by the time they got there, Eli was standing around as if nothing had happened, completely relaxed. The police had a word with him, and after a few minutes they pulled Sam to the side.

"I don't know what you guys are talking about, Sam," one of them said. "There's obviously nothing wrong here."

Sam told them what had just happened, but the police were still hesitant. Eli seemed so calm. He even came up and got involved in the conversation. But eventually they took him away. His wife came down to the house to talk to the officers, and they decided to admit him to a mental health facility.

When he was hospitalized, Eli started on some medication, which really seemed to help, until Sam told him that if he got his sins out and confessed, he wouldn't need the medicine. So he stopped taking his medicine and his mind started to go. Then he was back on his medicine, and he was doing better. Back and forth, back and forth.

One night, I found out Eli and his wife were gone. A few days later, Eli came back with a sheriff and a stock trailer, loaded up the last of his things, and left.

It was late fall when Eli Mullet left Bergholz, and the leaves were already off the trees.

4

JOINING THE CHURCH

I had turned seventeen that August, and in the spring I started taking instruction classes in order to join the Amish church in Bergholz. The community had dwindled. We were still having church—that would change within the year— but we were only communicating with one other Amish community. All the other neighboring Amish communities would have nothing to do with us. This kind of separation is unusual among the Amish—most of the time neighboring communities will mingle, share meals, and do business together. Their young people will hang out and date and eventually marry. But Bergholz was becoming more and more isolated. It was a strange feeling.

There were four or five of us in the instruction class we had to take before joining the church, and it was taught by the ministers—my grandfather Sam, Johnny Mullet, and Levi Miller—as well as Eli Hostetler, who was a deacon at the time.

Taking instruction classes is simple, and it lasts for eighteen weeks. Since church meets every other week, that's nine classes. The ministers take turns going over Bible verses and Amish rules and that sort of thing. We answer questions and are given things to think about. But the main thing happens during the third class, when they tell you the rules of the community. Then they give you a few weeks to think it over, because being baptized and joining the church is a big deal. It's a decision for life. If you decide to leave the church after you join, you'll be shunned. There's no way out of it. Of course, if you decide you want to rejoin, you can go back and repent, and after six weeks they'll let you rejoin the church.

But I didn't have any second thoughts. I had grown up in Bergholz. I had never imagined a future anywhere outside of it.

The day of my baptism into the church arrived. That particular church service is longer than a normal church service. Whoever is getting baptized sits on a special bench in front of the church. Normally in an Amish church service, women sit on one side and men on the other. On the day you get baptized, you sit in the very front row on the men's side. The service lasts an extra thirty or forty-five minutes.

For me, that morning was a big deal, but not so much because I was joining a church. For me it was a big deal because I was affirming my faith in front of a bunch of people. That part felt like a big deal, and as the ceremony took place, that's the aspect of it that made me a little emotional.

But there was also a part of the whole thing that made me a little anxious. When you get baptized, you have to promise to abide by the leaders' rules and the rules of their church. Repeating those things put me a little bit on edge.

I sat there quietly, and Sam, my grandfather, held his hands cupped over my head. The deacon of the church came along with a gallon bucket and a drinking cup, and he got water out of the bucket with the cup and poured it into the bishop's hands. I forget the exact words they used, but it was something like "In the name of the Father. The Son. And the Holy Spirit."

And with each of those three proclamations, the bishop released some of the water down on top of my head.

It was official. I was a member of the Bergholz Amish church.

At about the same time that I joined the church, there was a wedding in Bergholz. Weddings were rare in those days: we didn't have a lot of young folk to begin with, and now that a group of families had left and we weren't communicating with other Amish communities, weddings had become even rarer.

This wedding was a good wedding, and it was even better because a few of the young folks from a neighboring Amish community showed up for it. They were from Enon Valley, the only Amish community we were communicating with at the time. All in all, there were about six young people who attended the wedding: me, my brother, one of my cousins, and three girls from Enon Valley.

After a wedding, when you go in for dinner, the young folks couple up. I was paired with one of the girls from the valley. We talked all evening, hit it off really well, and started dating soon after that. I spent the next few weekends visiting her.

At about the same time, the folks in Enon Valley started having second thoughts about Bergholz. I guess ever since that meeting of the bishops, their community had been split about what to do with us. Should they ignore the fact that the Amish bishops had invalidated Sam's leadership? Should they continue in community with us? Or should they go along with everyone else who believed that something was seriously wrong in Bergholz?

And I had my own decisions to make: What was I going to do? I had just joined the church, and I didn't want to marry my new girlfriend and move to Enon Valley, because they were a different kind of Amish. They had different rules, and I liked things the way they were in Bergholz.

Things became more and more serious between us. She was kind and pretty, and I was getting close to the age when an Amish young man starts to think about his future—owning land, starting a family. One Sunday night, the girl from Enon Valley told me she thought she might be able to move to Bergholz, just so we could see each other more often. I was excited, and it felt as though my life was going in the direction I had always expected it to go.

She called me that week on the phone in Sam's barn and said she needed to talk. In person. I hired a driver (as I always had to do when making the forty-mile trek to Enon Valley) and went over to see her.

"I just don't know what to do," she said, on the verge of tears. "My mom doesn't want me to move to Bergholz. She's scared that our community will cut ties with you and that then I won't be able to see her anymore."

I couldn't stand to see her so upset, but it also frustrated me that she wasn't willing to make up her own mind. I see myself as an independent kind of guy—I do what I say I'm

going to do, and I don't usually let too many other people influence me. Those were hard days, and I found myself
thinking about her, thinking about our future, all the time.

We decided to wait and see what would happen.

"I'll see you next weekend," I said when I left. "Don't
worry. We'll talk about it then."

The folks at Enon Valley had church on a Wednesday
night, which is unusual. I don't know if it was specifically
to talk about the Bergholz situation or if there were other
things they wanted to discuss. On Friday night she called me
again. She didn't have good news.

"I don't think we should see each other anymore,"
she said.

"What? Why?"

"Too many people over here are talking. They don't think
I should be dating you because you're from Bergholz."

I was devastated.

"Why should you let what someone else thinks control what you do with your own life?" I asked her. "I just
don't understand."

She started crying. "I don't know," she said. "I feel like I
need to do whatever they tell me to do."

When we hung up that night, I couldn't see a way forward. I suddenly felt stuck in Bergholz, this church I had so
recently joined. Why had I done that? Why hadn't I waited
until I was a little older?

On Friday I went and talked to Sam about it. He and I
had been talking more ever since I joined the church. I think
he took special interest in the young men, because he knew

we were the future of Bergholz. I think he worried that if we left, everything he had built would fall apart.

"What should I do?" I asked him. "Should I keep dating her or what?"

My grandfather said he wasn't sure what I should do. It wasn't like Sam to not exert control of a situation. But I think, in some ways, his indecision was exactly how he controlled me. I think he knew Bergholz was becoming more and more isolated, and that I was probably still too young to do something like leave the community. So he sat back and let the situation unfold, and I imagine it went pretty much the way he thought it would go.

"Forget it," I said. "I don't care what those people think. I'm a man of my word, and I said I'd see her this weekend, so that's what I'm going to do."

I got a driver on Sunday morning, and my brother and I made the trek to Enon Valley. The whole way over there I was feeling nervous about what she would say when she saw me. Almost all the girls in Bergholz were my first cousins. Enon Valley was the only community still talking to Bergholz. If this didn't work out, I didn't know what I would do. Who would I marry? What kind of a future was there for me in Bergholz?

Everyone looked at us in a funny way when we got to the Enon Valley church that Sunday morning. Afterward I spoke with my girlfriend for a little bit.

"I'm sorry," she finally said. "I can't move to Bergholz. It's too isolated. I can't leave my church."

"If that's what you want," I said. "But I wanted to see you in person. I wanted to keep my word. That's why I'm here."

My brother and I left. The drive back to Bergholz had never felt so long. The road hummed under the tires. The

evening was dark and getting darker. I was choosing Bergholz over her, and I didn't even know why.

What had I done?

Not long after that, we found out that Enon Valley had
cut off all ties with Bergholz. We were completely isolated.
No other Amish communities wanted to have anything to do
with us. Those other communities considered Sam a rogue
bishop doing his own thing. Now I know that they were
right. Rumors about some of the things Sam was doing had
spread outside of our community.

I hadn't even heard those rumors yet, but I would
soon enough.

5

WRITING DOWN OUR SINS

After those families left Bergholz, after Eli Mullet's episodes passed and he left, after Enon Valley cut ties with us, things got quiet. Sam maintained a strong stance toward outsiders: everything they did was wrong, and everything we did was right. We circled the wagons, so to speak, and got on with our lives.

I worked a lot of hours, like most of the men in Bergholz, and I still lived with my parents. We went to church every other Sunday. We led quiet lives and prayed silent prayers before and after our meals. We turned off the gas lamps at night and fell asleep in the darkness, and when the sun came up, we got up and started a new day.

Maybe some of us thought the worst was behind us. Maybe it felt like a good time to take a deep breath and sigh with relief. I don't know. The fact was, Sam just couldn't let things be. He had to be in absolute control, 100 percent of the time.

If you met Sam today, you'd probably walk away thinking he was just about the nicest old man you ever met. That's
how he comes across. He's likeable and funny and interest-
ing to talk to. If you talked with him about the weather or
his family or his farm, you'd have an enjoyable time.

But if you asked him about Bergholz? If you questioned
his decisions or his motives? If you cast any doubt on the
things that took place there?

Then you'd see a different side of Sam Mullet.

I can't remember how it all started, people being asked to
write down their sins. I do remember at one point Sam asked
one young man to write down his sins and ended up using
that information against him. Maybe that's what started it
all. Maybe Sam realized the power he would have if he knew
everyone's secrets.

All I remember is that my mom and dad came home one
evening from Sam's place, and my mom told me that Sam
had said he wanted everyone to write down their sins. That
was the only way to make things right, to start over anew.

"Everyone?" I asked her.

"Everyone," she said.

I shrugged.

"If that's what he wants," I said. "I hope he doesn't freak
out when he reads everything I've done."

Over the next few days we received some clarification. I
can't remember if it was directly from Sam or if it was just
information passed through the grapevine. Apparently he
wanted us to go back as far as we could remember. Every little thing, even the smallest of sins. He even wanted to know
everyone's impure thoughts.

"This is how we get rid of sin," he said. "Confess your sins one to another."

Fine, I thought. *If that's what it takes.*

I sat down and wrote six pages, front and back, everything I could think of. I remembered stuff like lying or looking up an answer for my schoolwork when I wasn't supposed to. There were other things, things that were kind of embarrassing to write down.

At the end of the letter I signed my name and wrote two sentences.

You asked for everything. Here it is.

I guess Sam caught on that some of the men were hesitant about writing down their sins, so he approached them with a different proposition.

"How about this," he said. "Give me some money and it will pay for your sins."

One of the men, who happened to be one of his own sons, gave him $5,000. Another man gave him about the same amount. A third gave him $7,000 or $8,000, which Sam promptly took to Mount Hope, where he bought six or seven head of horses, all buggy horses. Then he had the gall to come back to Bergholz and try to sell one of those horses to one of the men who had given him the money!

"Nope," the other man said. "I already paid you once, Sam. I'm not paying you again. I'll take the horse, but I'm not giving you any more money."

Everyone in my family wrote down their sins for Sam. Every single person, including both of my parents. Even Sam's own wife, my grandmother, wrote down her sins and handed them to Sam. But he said he didn't believe her.

"Nope, that's not the truth," he said to her in front of everyone one day. "There's more. If you don't start telling me the truth, you're going to have to move out. You can't live in this house if you don't write everything down."

"Sam," my grandma said, "I already told you everything."

"No, you didn't," he said, not giving in. He went on to accuse her of all kinds of crazy things, including being with other men. Stuff none of us believed was true. But in the end my grandma promised Sam she would write everything down, and he relented.

This was in the late fall, maybe November or December. It was cold, and you could feel Christmas in the air, but there was something else, too, something hard to describe. I guess it was just this sense that something wasn't right.

My family loaded up in the buggy and headed to Sam's for Christmas. Most of the big community gatherings, for holidays or church meetings, were held at Sam's, and that year everyone was going to Sam's for a Christmas meal. We drove through the cold, the horses' breath steaming in the December air.

My dad and I hitched up the horses while the rest of my family carried things inside for the meal. As soon as I got inside I could feel the tension in the air. Something wasn't right.

Sam wasn't happy.

He met my family inside the door.

"You guys are going to have to leave because you didn't write the truth in your letters. You didn't write down all your sins."

This was Christmas Day. We all stood there, not knowing what to say.

"Grandma here," he said, beckoning toward his wife, "she's lying, too, so she's going to have to go home with you guys."

I knew my dad wouldn't be happy about that, for all kinds of different reasons, but mostly because our house was already packed full with the six of us kids. We didn't have a spare bed, much less a spare room. But of course we'd welcome my grandma if she needed a place to stay.

"We didn't lie, Sam," my dad said in a quiet voice. "But if you don't want us here, we're not going to stay."

There was an awkward moment when we didn't know exactly what to do. But then my family started gathering our things together, getting ready to go back out to the buggy and drive all the way home.

Sam spoke up again.

"Well, I guess Johnny can stay," he said, looking at me. "I think he's the only one who actually wrote down the truth."

I glanced at my parents, and they stared back at me. I kind of wanted to stay. After all, it was Christmas, and I could smell all the delicious food just waiting to be eaten:

My grandfather's farm in Bergholz.

ham, mashed potatoes, corn, and fresh rolls. I could hear the hum of conversation throughout the house. All our friends were there. Plus, for some reason, we all wanted Sam to like us, and the fact that he thought I had told the truth made me feel good.

I guess I felt kind of chosen, in a good way. I had recently gotten to the point where I was starting to like my grandfather. When I was little, his had always been the name invoked to threaten consequences for bad behavior, especially at school, where Sam's daughter (my aunt) was the teacher.

"Sam won't like it if you do that!"

"You'd better hope Sam doesn't find out about that!"

"You'll be in trouble when Sam hears you did that!"

So there I was, possibly winning his favor?

I stayed for dinner.

We ate a huge Christmas meal and then sat around and talked until it started getting dark outside. I hung out with my cousins and had a good time. As night settled in, Sam pulled me aside.

"You can stay for a couple of days, if you want," he offered. "It would be nice to have you around."

It felt good to know that my grandfather believed me, but it seemed like an odd request. I knew my parents depended on me for things at the house, and if I didn't go home it would mean more work for them. Plus, I had never lived away from home before. My youngest aunt, Lizzie, came in and talked to me. We had been born on the same day, and she had always felt more like my sister or cousin than an aunt.

"Why don't you stay for a couple of days?" she asked.

Lizzie and I talked for a little bit, and I thought about it. I decided I'd stay for a week and then go home.

That's not exactly how it worked out.

6

WHEN WE PUT
OUR BIBLES AWAY

The first week in Sam's house during the Christmas season was a confusing time for me. I missed my family. I missed my dad and wondered how he was getting on with all the work at home.

But by the end of the week, Sam had said so many bad things about my mom and dad that I didn't want to go home anymore. He told me stories about things that had happened years before, things my dad had done, and it scared me. It was confusing for me to hear this stuff about my parents, but I didn't have any reason to think Sam might not be telling the truth. What I didn't realize was that was how Sam operated: he used knowledge and emotions and sometimes lies to drive a wedge between people.

Isolated people, it turns out, are very easy to control.

After hearing Sam's revelations about my family, I suddenly felt as though I didn't even know my parents. I didn't know what to do.

"You could always move in here with me, if you need some more time before you go home," Sam suggested, and I took him up on it. The idea of being independent appealed to me, and I was still coming to grips with all the stuff I had learned about my parents. Whether my grandfather's stories were true or not—well, I didn't know. I wasn't sure who to believe anymore. I figured I'd make a go of it on my own. Sure, it was Sam's place, but it felt like somewhere I could go, at least until I worked through some of this in my mind.

I talked to my parents about moving to Sam's house, and they weren't happy about it. But at the end of the conversation, they sort of gave in. I didn't want to tell them all the things I had heard about them, and I can't remember exactly the reasons I gave for moving to Sam's. But in the end, I moved there and started helping him on his construction crew, which was run by my uncle Johnny Mullet.

As is the case with most Amish households, the head of the household collects the wages of any of his children who have jobs and still live at home. In other words, Sam got all my money. So from the age of seventeen to twenty-one, instead of my dad getting my paycheck, Sam got it because I lived under his roof.

But even that wasn't quite normal. Usually if an Amish kid is giving his wages to his parents, his parents take care of his needs, like new clothes or shoes or supplies for his horses. Yet when I went to Sam and asked for a new pair of work boots, he just grunted.

"Go ask your dad," he said, without looking me in the eye.

I felt stupid asking my dad. But I needed boots and didn't want to press Sam about it, so I gave in and asked my dad.

"Hey, Dad," I said when I saw him one day around the community. "I need some new work boots."

My dad looked up at me with a strange look on his face.

"Doesn't Sam have your money?" he asked me.

I shrugged.

"I don't know what he's doing with it," I said. "All I know is that I need a new pair of boots, and he told me to ask you."

My dad stared at me for a moment and then gave me some cash. He didn't say a word. The fact that my dad had to pay for my stuff while Sam collected my check: that wasn't right. I think back on those days and have to shake my head at the things that went on. I can't believe I went along with some of that stuff. I can't believe I was giving all my money to Sam and then asking my dad to buy me things.

Winter broke and spring swept into Bergholz. The fields were tilled and brown, and the forest started to turn green. Construction work picked up as the ground thawed, and the whole community became so busy that we didn't have time to think about the strange things that had happened the year before.

We cut the hay and put it up. We planted oats and then threshed the oats. But when winter rolled around again, when we settled in for the long dark season, that's when all the strange things seemed to happen. Always in the winter.

It was about that time that Sam decided we shouldn't have church anymore.

"Maybe we'd better not pray anymore either," he said. "Not before or after meals, not in the morning or evening."

I don't know that anyone said anything in reply. We were all shocked by his decision not to have church. None of us had ever even imagined a world where we wouldn't go to church! It was part of our heritage, part of our life. We were dedicated to following God, and it was hard to understand how *not* having church was a good thing. But Sam said it, so we listened.

"And put your Bibles away," he added. "The devil is twisting things around. He's twisting the way people are reading the words and confusing people."

So we all put our Bibles away, and that was that.

Everyone was getting scared. There was a sense of desperation to make things right with God. Why else were these crazy things happening, if not that God was unhappy with us?

7

THE DEMONS IN SAM'S BARN

In my grandfather Sam Mullet's world, there were always lines, mostly between those he said were living right and those who weren't. There were the Good Guys, and there were the Bad Guys, and Sam had a way of keeping the two groups very well defined. I don't think he ever used the terms "Good Guys" or "Bad Guys," but we always knew who was in and who was out.

Sam decided a group of guys, about seven or eight of the men in Bergholz, were clearly the Bad Guys. He started laying down the law for them and dishing out punishments.

"Maybe then you'll start writing all your sins down," he told them.

Sometimes Sam had them do work for him, things like clearing the service roads in the woods around his house or mucking out his stalls. Other times he punished them by making them go live in a chicken coop or in the stables. When they lived in the chicken coop, they ate food from the scraps thrown in for the chickens. A few of the men rubbed chicken poop into their hair to show remorse. Whether it was chores or punishment, it was all designed, according to Sam, to help them "pay for their sins"—sins they sometimes hadn't even committed—and to get them to be sorry for not telling the truth.

People became very serious about trying to rid themselves of these sins, which Sam had brought to the forefront when he made all of us write them down. The men went into the chicken coops and the stalls willingly. The days were getting shorter, and the nights were growing cold and dark.

One of the men who spent time in a chicken coop was Eli Miller. He was over at Freeman Burkholder's chicken coop. I was still living in Sam's house at this time. I was there when it happened.

He sent word that he wanted Eli to come down to his house, and when Eli got there he looked awful. He had been in that chicken coop for two weeks or so without having a shower. He was dirty, and small pieces of straw stuck out from his beard. I think Sam wanted to talk with Eli because Eli's wife had moved in with Sam while Eli was in the coop, and I guess some things had come up that Sam wanted to talk to him about.

"First things first, we need to get you cleaned up," Sam said. "Go take a shower."

Eli came back to the kitchen, clean, but he hadn't shaved yet. He had dark hair, jet black, and he was maybe six feet tall, well built. Sam wanted me to clean him up, so I used the scissors and a razor to do that.

"Why don't you take his whole beard off," Sam suggested. "I tell you what: give him one of those beards around his mouth."

"Like a Fu Manchu?" I asked.

"Yeah," Sam said. "One of those. And give him a crew cut."

I shrugged. I had never cut anyone's hair like that before. I tried to use my fingers as a guide for the clippers.

Eli smiled the whole time. He thought it was kind of funny, and I think he was glad to be out of the coop.

"This is another chance at *rumspringa*," he joked, referring to that time in an Amish person's life when they do things they're not allowed to do. The three of us laughed.

I gave him a decent haircut, and he looked like an attorney or something. I don't know. I'd never seen an Amishman who looked the way Eli did. Later, when Sam had me give more haircuts, some of the guys came out looking cleaner, better, but other guys looked like someone you'd be scared to meet up with on the street.

Soon an idea started floating around. I don't know exactly where the idea came from, but someone suggested that one way to make things right with God would be for more people to cut their hair and beards. By humbling ourselves and cutting our hair, we could be cleansed of our sins. Such haircuts would be symbols, a kind of cleansing humiliation as well as a fresh start.

That was the winter four of the women in our community had their hair shaved off. Two of my aunts gave the haircuts, and the four women to receive them were my mom, my grandmother (Sam's wife), Johnny Mullet's wife, and Lester Miller's wife. They quit wearing coverings and instead wore headscarves to hide their bald heads.

I had never seen an Amish woman with hair that short, and seeing my mother after she had her hair cut sent a shiver through me. Something wasn't right in Bergholz. Something felt as if it was getting out of control. Whenever I caught a glimpse of my mother's bare scalp under her headscarf, it filled me with an uneasy feeling.

We started meeting at Sam's house every night from around eight until midnight. The whole community was there. That's when I started to notice that the wives of the men in the chicken coops lived with Sam. There were three or four women living there by then. Their husbands knew something was going on, but no one wanted to confront Sam about it.

None of it made any sense. None of it seemed right. But it all started small, and in the beginning it made sense. The men were willing to go into the coops to pay for their sins. What were their wives going to do? Live at home alone? So when they first moved in with Sam, no one said anything. You learned to look the other way. You learned to ignore the voices in your head that were telling you, *This isn't right. None of this is right.*

"You're not fessing up to your sins," Sam continued to say to the men. "You're not being honest about the bad things you've done," he'd say, with warning in his voice.

At the same time, there were the Good Guys who, for whatever reason, had gotten on Sam's good side. I was one of them. My uncle Crist was in this group with me, along with Raymond Miller, Ferdinand Miller, Lester Mullet, and a few of my cousins. Sam would egg us on to tell the Bad Guys what they were supposed to be doing. This is where it came to me doing things I really regret.

Sam came up with the craziest ideas, and those of us who were the Good Guys would grab on to whatever they were and run with them. The Bad Guys would get scared of the punishments and shrink back like little kids. We blamed them for things they never did, and they denied the charges. But Sam wanted us to keep insisting until finally they owned up to it all and took their punishment.

It was sick.

He had the Bad Guys so confused and mixed up about what they had done and what they hadn't done that they didn't know how to respond. We Good Guys, on the other hand, listened to Sam, and I guess we listened for many different reasons. We liked being on Sam's side. We liked being in the crowd that was telling people what to do, and we knew that if we didn't listen we'd end up in the Bad Guy crowd. We wanted Sam to approve of us. The Bad Guys spent a couple of weeks living in the barn, sleeping in the animal stalls. Sometimes Sam would let them come inside to eat, but usually one of us Good Guys would take food out to them.

Anyway, the Bad Guys didn't know which end was up.

My dad was one of the Bad Guys.

One Saturday evening Sam told the Bad Guys he had some work for them to do. Monday was deer season and there were a lot of logging roads that needed to be cleared to make hunting easier.

"I guess if you guys clear those logging roads then we can all go hunting on Monday," Sam said. I could tell it lifted everyone's spirits. I think they all hoped that maybe their time of living in the barn was coming to an end.

So he got them all fired up, and come Sunday morning, as soon as the sun was up, the Bad Guys took some chainsaws and pitchforks and went out into the woods to cut the briars and clear the trails. They worked all day Sunday, from sunup to sundown, so they could go hunting on Monday. It makes me shake my head now to think of how much had changed in such a short time: that eight Amish men would go out into the woods on a Sunday and work. I don't think I had ever worked on a Sunday in my life, except maybe for milking cows.

On Sunday night, Sam told them to come into the house. They all sat there on the bench after dinner, one after the other in a long row. I could see they were wiped out, totally exhausted, and the eight of them sat there with their heads hanging. As I said, they hadn't been getting much food, and they'd been sleeping in the barn, and I think that long day of hard work clearing trails had really taken it out of them.

Someone said something, something that was sort of the beginning of everything that would happen in the next couple of years.

"You know, I think these guys need a haircut."

I don't even remember who suggested it first. My stomach sank, because there was my dad, sitting there, hanging his head, looking absolutely beat. The dad I had left in order to move in with Sam. The dad who used to take me mushroom hunting. The dad who gave me a love of horses.

A few of the women came along with scissors and just went right down the row of eight men, chopping their beards off in one fell swoop. Not trimming them nice and even—no, they just took fistfuls in their hands and cut those beards square along the bottom. Everything was uneven and all disheveled. It looked awful, terrible.

Sam turned to the Good Guys. "Why don't you guys go ahead and trim their beards up a little bit, fix them up."

A few of the Good Guys started cutting and snipping, but they didn't know what they were doing. They were only making it worse, and when they saw they were making it worse, they laughed and didn't even try anymore.

Levi Miller, a minister and one of the Good Guys, had grown up with my dad. He and my dad had done a lot of mischievous things together when they were younger, and they had each written down their own version of those events when Sam told everyone to write down their sins. When their two versions didn't match up exactly, Sam went back and forth between the two, telling them what the other had said they had done and asking for more information. Sam really put a wall between Levi and my dad, a wall that led to a lot of anger and tension.

Now, in the kitchen, Levi smirked. "I want to cut Johnny's dad's beard," Levi said. "And I want to cut his hair, too."

I started to feel sick. Things were getting weird. I felt Sam looking at me.

Levi Miller, a minister and one of the "Good Guys."

"C'mon, Johnny, cut off some of your dad's hair," Sam said to me, smiling. "You're mad at him too, aren't you?"

I shrugged but didn't make a move.

"Oh, come on," Sam said in a good-natured tone, as if we were talking about the weather. "You need to cut some of his hair off too."

I could barely breathe. But I stood up slowly and took the scissors from Levi. I walked over to my dad and stood in front of him. Everyone else in the room was silent. It's pretty similar to how I felt later, in the courtroom at Sam's trial.

Amish boys are trained from an early age to respect their elders, and especially their fathers. We listen to our dads and will do whatever they say, sometimes even when it doesn't make sense. Until I had moved into Sam's house at the age of seventeen, I had never done anything to openly disrespect my father.

But there I stood, the scissors in my hand. Everyone stared at me, waiting to see what I would do.

I reached out and took a small piece of my dad's hair in between my fingers and cut. The sound grated down to my bones. I took another small chunk and cut it off. And another.

Levi stood up loudly behind me.

"Here," he said, "I'll finish this up."

He pushed me aside, and I sat back down, shaken to the core.

"I'm going to give him a backward Mohawk," Levi said.

Instead of cutting my dad's hair off the side the way they had with the others, Levi cut a big trail right up the middle. My dad didn't even make a move. He just sat there and waited, his shoulders slumped. I can only imagine what he must have been feeling.

Me? I don't remember feeling very much at the time. It was as if everything was happening in a haze, or a dream. Looking back now, it's hard to believe I ever would have done such a thing.

It was midnight by the time the Bad Guys trudged back out to the barn to sleep. They looked awful. Bright and early Monday morning, they were up again and working around Sam's farm. I think they were trying to get some of the work finished before it was time to go hunting.

The Good Guys, including me, walked out to the barn with Sam in the early morning light. Sam just stood there for a moment. Then he told us to let the Bad Guys know the news. He had changed his mind.

"They can't go deer hunting after all," Sam said.

That was all he said.

I walked out the driveway with the rest of the Good Guys after the news had been delivered, all of us holding our guns. I stared down toward the barn and caught a glimpse of the Bad Guys. It scared me to look at them. The ones who didn't have their hats on, I could see their hair, and they looked like mad men, like wild animals. The ones who did have their hats on—well, their hats were far too big now that they didn't have hair. Those hats sat crooked and loose. It looked as if their heads had shrunk. Their faces were gaunt and black from weariness. They hadn't shaved in weeks, so they had hair growing on their necks and faces. They hadn't showered for weeks, either. None of them were smiling.

I looked down there as I walked by and I thought, *If they don't look like a whole bunch of demons.*

I kept on walking and I didn't look back.

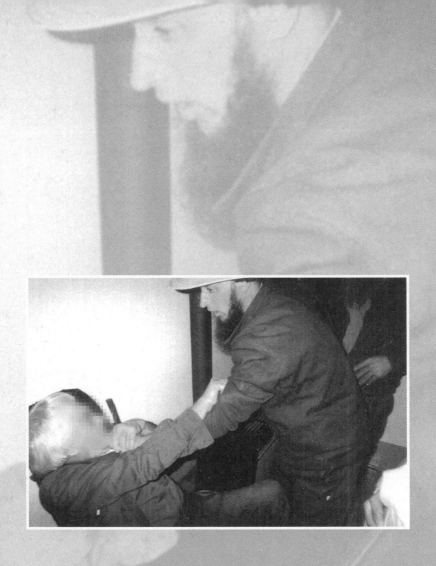

One of the beard-cutting attacks that was caught on camera.

PART II
The Beard Cutters

8

HE STARTED SCREAMING

The prosecuting attorney stood in front of me.

"Did there come a time you heard members of the Bergholz community talking about cutting the head and beard hair of Amish people who lived outside of the community?" she asked.

"Yes," I said quietly, trying to keep my gaze from wandering around the courtroom. I needed to stay focused. I wanted to say the right thing.

"When did you first start hearing talk of those types of beard and hair cuttings?" the prosecuting attorney asked me.

"Approximately two years ago."

"And where did you hear these discussions take place?"

"Mostly out in the barn when all the men were there."

"And who was being discussed as potential candidates for having their hair and beards cut?"

"The only ones I can recall right now would be Martin and Barbara Miller."

"And so those were the discussions that started about two years ago?"

"Yes."

"And who was talking about cutting the head and beard hair of Marty and Barb Miller?"

"Her children," I said.

But I didn't think of the Millers in that moment. I thought about cutting my own father's hair, and about the way I had taken those small locks in my fingers and chopped them off. I thought of the sound the scissors made as they chewed through.

I took another deep breath. It felt as if I had been on the stand for hours, but I knew I still had a long way to go.

"Which ones specifically did you hear talking about it?"

"I remember hearing Marty and Allen talking about it."

"Marty and Allen?"

"Yes."

"Anyone else?"

I tried to remember the scene, now already so far in the past. "Lester might have said something about it."

Although I tried not to, I couldn't help but glance over at Lester Miller. He was staring at the floor.

"And what was . . . and was there a reason given for why they might want to do this?"

I remembered what they had said. "Yes."

"And what was that?"

"The way they had raised their children."

She asked me more about that, and I tried to remember the late-night conversations I had overheard in the barn, the conversations that had come before the beard cuttings.

"And in view of that, what was . . . what did the Millers say would be helpful or . . . let me rephrase that. Why did the Millers think that cutting the hair or beards of their parents would be a means of addressing this?"

I wasn't sure what she meant. "Could you ask that again?"

"Yes. It was not a very good question. Why . . . you've described what the Miller parents were doing . . . that the children didn't like. Why did they want to address that by cutting their hair and beards?"

"Objection," one of the defense lawyers stated.

"Sustained," the judge said, glancing around the room.

The prosecuting attorney reworded the question.

"What was cutting the hair and beards of the Miller parents supposed to accomplish?"

"Objection." Again, one of the defense lawyers spoke up.

"I think we've covered this," the judge said in an annoyed tone of voice.

The prosecuting attorney tried one more time. "Did any of the members of the Miller family tell you that they had discussed cutting their father's beard with Sam Mullet, Senior?"

"Objection," Sam's attorney said in a loud voice.

"Overruled," the judge said.

"Yes," I said.

"They said they did discuss it with him?"

"Yes."

"All right. Directing your attention to September the 6th of 2011 and the beard cuttings that did take place with respect to Marty and Barb Miller: did you know that was going to happen in advance?"

I nodded. "Only about ten minutes in advance," I said.

"All right. So ten minutes before they left, describe that for us. When did you learn that this was going to happen?"

"It would have been the evening they did it," I said. "They pulled in the driveway, said they're going to go do it."

"All right. When you say they pulled into the driveway, which driveway?"

"Sam Mullet's driveway."

"And where . . . who did you speak to and where were you when you spoke to them?"

"I spoke with all the men, and I was upstairs in the apartment."

"So the Millers were upstairs in the apartment?"

"Yes," I said.

"What happened after they came inside?"

"They told us what they did; that was about it."

"Well, what did they say they had done?"

I paused. "They said that they had gotten their father out of bed, cut his hair . . . his beard off and that the ladies had cut Barbara's hair off."

"And what did they say about how their father, Marty Miller, reacted?"

I remembered how they had told the story. I remembered how his own children had been laughing while they told us about it.

"He started screaming," I said in a quiet voice.

9

TURNING
THE TABLES

The Bad Guys were not happy when Sam didn't let them hunt, especially after they had done all of that work to clear the forest. But I think they were so worn out that they didn't have much fight left in them. They had all sort of resigned themselves to their fate, and they were all waiting for the end, whenever that might come.

Sam didn't let them go out with us on Tuesday either. He simply left them directions on the work he wanted them to do around the house. He continued to banish some of them to the chicken coops.

A lot of people ask me the same question, especially about those days in particular: Why would a bunch of grown men allow another man to treat them that way? I can't say for sure, but I think that for most of us, Bergholz was all we had. Every friend we had in the world lived there, every family member we cared about at the time. And Sam held the key to all of that. No one wanted to be banished from

Bergholz. No one wanted to lose everything. I think some of them also felt that doing all of these things was honestly a way for them to pay for their sins.

But you also have to understand that our beliefs as Amish people meant that Sam, as the church bishop, had a lot of power over our eternal souls. The rules he put in place were the final words. If we didn't listen to him—well, I think most of us truly believed that we'd be putting our eternity in jeopardy.

By the time Wednesday of that week rolled around, Sam decided the Bad Guys would be allowed to join us when we went hunting but that they couldn't bring their guns. Their job was to run through the brush and chase the deer out of hiding. That would drive the game toward us. We Good Guys took our guns and walked into one part of the woods, while the other men went in at a different point and then walked toward us, through the briars and the underbrush.

On Friday and Saturday, Sam finally let them bring their guns out, and everyone's spirits rose. By Saturday evening, even the Bad Guys were feeling better about life, a little upbeat. They still had their crazy hair and chopped-up beards, but it felt as though the strange stuff might be behind us. Maybe we could get back to being a normal community.

Late that Saturday afternoon, just as it was getting dark, Emanuel Shrock came into Sam's house. He was really animated. I don't know why, but Emanuel was wearing a belt with a plastic pistol strapped to it and a hat that looked like a cowboy hat. He started prancing around the place, acting like a bad guy in a Western. We all kind of laughed when we saw him.

All of us, that is, except my uncle Crist. Something about what Emanuel was doing set Crist off. He sat there getting more and more mad. He was steaming. Crist had a bushy red beard, maybe eight to ten inches long, and he was one of the few men who never had any part of his beard cut. Emanuel and Crist had a long-standing feud, and before anyone knew what was happening, Crist grabbed Emanuel and threw him to the ground.

"I'm going to tie that sucker up and drag him down the road behind my buggy," Crist declared. We all laughed and jumped up, holding Emanuel down until Crist could get a rope. Emanuel struggled like a wild animal. He was a well-built guy, maybe around 170 pounds or so, and he was difficult to keep down. His feet were flying everywhere, and he lashed out. One of his swings landed, and he punched Lester Mullet right in the mouth.

Lester cried out and walloped Emanuel several times in the face, and Emanuel went kind of limp. Crist got even more angry after Emanuel punched Lester. I guess he thought Emanuel should just lie there and take his medicine. So he tied a little rope around Emanuel's feet and dragged him outside, down a few concrete steps. Emanuel's head thudded against each step on the way down, and I thought he was probably unconscious by then. Things escalated so quickly. I don't know if I was worried about what was going on or not. It was all a blur, all happening so fast.

Crist went back into Sam's house to get his coat. It was a cold autumn day outside, and a cool breeze had kicked up after the sun went down. Everyone was worked up from the fight, and Lester was still holding his mouth from where Emanuel had clocked him. We all walked back out with him to watch what would happen next, but when we got out there,

Emanuel was gone. All that was left was a little blood in the white snow. Somehow he had untied himself and run off.

Sam had been there with us, watching the whole time.

"I guess you need to be a little more careful," he said, and then turned and went back inside the house. I don't know if he meant we should be more careful about hurting each other or if we should have been more careful and not let Emanuel get away.

Crist, Lester, and I went looking for Emanuel. I was concerned that he was either seriously hurt, lying out there in the cold somewhere, or else getting a gun and preparing to shoot someone. We searched and searched, late into the night, and no one found him.

"I'm going to bed," Crist announced abruptly. It felt like total chaos, like there was no idea what would happen next.

During the night, Emanuel showed up at his own house. I guess he had been hiding out in the woods while we searched for him. He warmed up a bit and then surrendered. A few of the Good Guys put him in a box stall inside the barn. I guess they were worried that he might call the sheriff, and we had enough trouble going on at the time without getting the police involved.

I remember that they chained Emanuel's ankles together and chained him to the wall. Now he was one of the Bad Guys.

There was another man in the community whose name was Freeman Burkholder. He wasn't one of the guys living down in the barn. He had a deer-processing business, and it kept him very busy in the winter during deer season. Because his business was outside of town and because he was so busy, I think he thought he had avoided all the hair and beard cutting that was taking place in Bergholz that winter.

But Levi Miller and Raymond Miller had other ideas.

"We're going to shave that guy totally bald," they said to Sam and me one afternoon, and that's exactly what they did.

The two of them went to Freeman's business while he was working and they cut off his hair and his beard and then totally shaved him. He came into Sam's place that Sunday night, and I didn't even recognize him at first. He looked plenty sheepish and tried to laugh it off. Everyone else laughed with him, but I had never seen anything like it.

There was snow that winter, and then there was rain, and then there was cold. And the snow wasn't deep after that, but what was left had a thick crust of ice on it. When you walked, your feet broke through in chunks. For a few days all the trees around Bergholz were coated in ice. The sky was a whitish gray, and the days were short.

My cousin Melvin, one of my best friends, got pulled into the group of Bad Guys after he didn't do everything he was supposed to do. Because Melvin didn't do his part, my brother Edward had to do a lot more, and some of the guys complained about him to Sam.

"Gang up on him," Sam told Edward. "Go down to the barn and drag him up here, and we'll see what's going on."

Edward went down to the place where everyone was staying, and he got three or four guys together. They ganged up on Melvin, put a rope around his feet, and dragged him up to Sam's place. Literally dragged him, through the ice and snow. It was maybe half a mile, and he didn't have a coat on or anything—just a normal shirt. But since they were dragging him by his feet, his shirt slid up under his shoulders and he rode on his bare stomach on the crusted snow.

They let him loose up at Sam's house, and Melvin's mom was right there. She had her own issues at the time. Well, Melvin sort of stood up, a little wobbly, and he spit in his mother's face, as if to say, "Are you happy now? Is this what you wanted?"

She walked away. She didn't even say a word.

Melvin stood there quietly for a few minutes, standing still. The other guys all laughed and left the house. I guess they thought they had made things even. But I was right there beside him.

"My chest kind of hurts," Melvin said quietly, standing still.

Then he turned gingerly and walked out to the mudroom, getting ready to leave. I followed him to the door.

"Johnny, my chest hurts really bad," he whispered.

"Pull up your shirt," I said.

He pulled it up slowly so that I could look. His whole chest was lacerated from the ice and snow, covered in blood. It looked awful.

Holy cow, I thought to myself. But I tried not to react because I didn't want him to get scared.

"Wait a minute," I told him.

I walked back through the house until I found Sam.

"Sam," I said. "Come here."

He came back out with me, and I pulled up Melvin's shirt.

"Oh boy," he said, sighing. "We've got to get that cleaned up."

I took care of Melvin and put some bandages on him. I gave him one of my coats, and he went back to the house where he was staying. I watched him walk away, his feet breaking through the thin layer of ice and snow.

Every four or five days, Melvin came up to Sam's and I helped him wash out the wounds and put on some new bandages. It was another case of not wanting to go to the outside world for help because no one wanted the attention that might bring. We had become so isolated from the outside world that we didn't know which end was up.

That entire time in Bergholz was just stupid thing after stupid thing like that. It was an isolated community completely out of control. It's hard for me to imagine now that Edward and I and some of Melvin's other friends would do things like that to each other. To our own family!

But at the end of the day, we stuck together. The only thing I can say is that because we all went through it, we really understand each other now. And maybe that's what it took to get us out—a series of awful experiences that we shared—because eventually we all decided to leave together. I don't know. I hope some good came of Bergholz.

At some point during that November and December, Sam had put Levi Miller in charge of the Bad Guys, and he worked them hard. The only thing Levi gave them to eat and drink was a glass of water and a piece of bread in the morning and in the evening. Sometimes Sam would give them a few pieces of deer bologna. This went on for weeks, and the men in the barn were getting weak. My dad was still one of those men in the barn.

One day the men went up to Sam's house.

"We can't take it anymore, Sam," they told him. "We're getting weak and hungry."

"Why?" Sam asked. "What are you eating?"

"Levi is cutting our slices of bread thinner and thinner every day, and he gives us less and less water. Yet he expects us to work harder. We can't take it anymore."

Sam nodded.

"I didn't realize how bad it was," Sam said sympathetically, once again redirecting the blame to someone else. "Listen, when Levi comes home from work tonight, you guys pile on him and tell him how it is. You don't have to put up with this."

The men looked encouraged.

"You guys take the house and put him in the barn," Sam said, laughing, pleased with his idea. "See how he likes it then!"

Sometime that afternoon Sam pulled Crist and me aside. "Listen," he said. "When Levi gets back tonight, I'd like to know what happens. Maybe the two of you could hide out there and watch?"

So Crist and I spied on them while all of this happened.

Levi got home that night and came over to Sam's place. He called for the guys in the barn, the Bad Guys, but no one came out. Sam was outside with him. "What's going on?" he asked Sam.

Sam shrugged. "I don't know," he said. "Maybe you'd better go down there to the barn and get them."

Levi went storming down to the barn. I think he was probably going to give them all kinds of heck for not coming out when he called for them. But the barn was empty. He looked around for a few minutes before coming back outside. I saw him stare up at the house and the lights were on.

The Bad Guys were all up there at the house. They had shaved and showered and gotten cleaned up. The atmosphere in there was like some long-awaited celebration. They had even made themselves a big dinner and were devouring it when Levi entered the house.

All those seven or eight men stood up in a line and listened to Levi while he shouted at them up and down, telling them what chores they needed to do and who was going to do what and how dare they leave the barn without his permission. Didn't they know who was in charge? Didn't they know who was calling the shots? The Bad Guys didn't wait long, though. They piled on top of him, tied him up, carried him outside, and threw him into the barn.

When they came back to Sam's house, they were laughing and patting each other on the back, and they all sat back down and ate more food. They were finally having fun, too, and I could tell they felt good about life.

Through all of this—through the violence and the intimidation, the haircuts and the changes we couldn't understand, the odd punishments and the penance—through all of it, Sam sat there and watched. As I reflect on what happened, I believe that Sam orchestrated it, and he controlled us all, and that gave him the power to sometimes just sit and watch it all play out. He split up families, maybe because it forced everyone to rely on him. He pitted the strongest men against each other, and they couldn't direct their energy at him or the things he was doing because they were all fighting with each other. When the weak or the punished got fed up, he flipped the tables, and they felt thankful to him for doing it, as though he was doing them some huge favor. As though he was some kind of savior.

He was the bishop of our community. He was the grandfather to everyone—if not your actual grandfather, then at least a grandfather figure. He let these things happen.

10

MY GRANDFATHER'S POWER

I was a young man at the time, nineteen years old, and one of the aspects of being a strict Amish community, in the case of Bergholz, was that we practiced what's called a hands-off courtship. That means that if two young people go out on a date, they don't touch. They don't kiss. They don't even hold hands. Those were the rules, and I had committed to those rules when I joined the church. A hands-off courtship.

During that crazy winter, when the Bad Guys lived in the barn and Melvin got dragged through the snow, Sam approached me for a favor.

"I'm heading out to do a little deer hunting tomorrow," he told me. "Would you sight in my gun for me?"

"Sure," I said.

"Okay, I'll leave it out on the kitchen table for you. You can do it in the morning."

The next morning, I woke up early and fed the horses, then turned back toward the house. I walked through the dark morning and went inside, but the gun wasn't on the kitchen table. I figured Sam must have forgotten to leave it out, so I crept quietly through the house to his bedroom. I knew he kept his gun cabinet with all his guns in there. I could go in real quiet and take it out, get it sighted for him, and then he could still hunt that morning.

I opened the door and peered into the darkness. Light from the hall spilled into the room. There he was, in bed with his daughter-in-law.

My word. I was shocked.

I grabbed the gun before backing out of there so fast I nearly fell over. I shook my head in disbelief the entire way. I went back out to the barn and sat there, a million questions running through my mind.

Later that day, Sam and I crossed paths.

"I apologize," he said, but he didn't apologize for what I thought he was going to apologize for. "I forgot to put my gun out. I'm sorry."

"That's okay," I said, brushing it off. "But help me under-stand something. How can you as the bishop of Bergholz say you're going to help me with my problems when you're sleeping with your daughter-in-law? I mean, you expect me to practice a hands-off courtship, but you're sleeping with other women?"

To be honest, by then we all suspected that kind of thing was going on. But to walk in and see him sharing his bed with someone besides my grandmother? That blew me away.

"I'm sorry to confuse you like that," Sam said in his quiet, understanding voice. He could be very convincing when he spoke like that. "I really am. And, Johnny, I can't explain it. I can't."

Then he said something I'll never forget. "Somehow, I'm getting a lot of power by committing these sins. I know it's wrong, but I'm getting a lot of power."

I can be sarcastic sometimes, especially when I get angry.

"Okay," I said, "if you can get all that power, how about you let me try it? How about I get some of that power too?"

He stomped off, and after that he didn't want to talk to me about it anymore. If the subject ever did come up, we argued about it and both got angry.

It was after that when I moved out to the apartment above his shop. He didn't want me living in the house with him and the women who were there at the time. I was glad to be out of the house. I was glad to have my own place.

That whole winter was nonstop chaos and drama. I think a lot about the poor little kids who grew up during that time. So many of the men were in the barn or the chicken coop, and so many of the women were being taken advantage of by Sam. Who took care of the children? Who took care of the wives who didn't give in to Sam? It was so messed up. Never will those kids be like little children in a normal home. They didn't have a mom or dad for months at a time. I just can't think about it. They lost their innocence.

Eventually spring came around, and I got out the clippers and every evening for a few weeks we had a barber stool set up. I trimmed the beards and hair of the men whose beards were cut and gave them all haircuts, and everyone looked decent. The women who had their heads shaved—well, their hair was beginning to grow out too. I figured that within a year or two you wouldn't be able to even see that any of it had happened.

Yet there were still reminders. Emanuel had bruises on the side of his face from where he had been beaten up. Every so often I found something in the barn that reminded me of the men who had been forced to live there for most of the winter.

I think most of us felt a sense of relief that the winter was behind us. Now we could put our hands to hard work in the spring and summer and fall. Maybe things would get better in Bergholz. But what we didn't realize was that everything that took place that winter was just a glimpse of what would happen a year and a half later. Sam had gotten a taste for what it felt like to make people pay, to make people say they were sorry. It wouldn't be long before he'd turn his attention to those people outside of Bergholz who had wronged him.

One of the main ways to know that spring had arrived in Bergholz was that we all started making trips to the auction to purchase livestock, horses, farming equipment, or just to get out of the community and rub shoulders with other folks and hear the news of the world. As spring started to thaw things out and the snow melted, we began making those regular trips and bringing back the things we needed.

Sam realized, after a few trips to the auction, that there were already rumors flying around about Bergholz. The chief rumor was that we, as a community, were going to leave the Amish. The reason people were saying that was because so many of us showed up at the auction that spring with beards and hair that had been cut. I think everybody there expected us to start buying trucks and mechanized farming equipment.

"I'm going to prove them wrong," Sam muttered to me one night before going to the machine auction the next morning. He took a couple of guys with him and proceeded to pay outrageous amounts of money for horse-drawn farming equipment, just to prove to people that we were still Amish. It was money I don't think he had at that time, but he was determined to control what people were saying about Bergholz.

It was an uneventful summer. I worked hard, kept my head down, and my cousins and I did our own thing. Four of us were living in the apartment above Sam's shop by that time, and he was lenient with us. We didn't always dress the way we should, and sometimes we played music in the barn. But Sam never pressed those issues with us. I think he was worried about us leaving, and he knew that if he came down too hard on us, we would, unlike our elders, leave Bergholz before anyone knew what had happened.

Then winter came and went—the first uneventful winter in a few years. There was no Eli losing his mind, no Bad Guys in the barn. There weren't any hair or beard cuttings or men living in chicken coops. It was a quiet winter, and it almost felt as though things were getting back to normal. We still weren't having church though. Every so often the community would hang out at Sam's, but for the most part everyone did their own thing.

The following summer, things were still slow. I went to work during the day and came home to work Sam's farm at night. The crops came in nicely, and it looked as if it would be a good harvest.

Toward the end of the summer, we had the binder out and were cutting up the oats, getting ready to thresh them. I was working with Eli Miller, and he seemed very withdrawn.

"What's wrong?" I finally asked him. "What is your problem?"

"I don't want to talk about it," he said in a firm voice.

"Fine," I said, "but you can't just walk around here acting like this."

I gave him a hard time about it, and he interrupted me, staring me right in the eyes.

"If you knew what was wrong—if it were you—you wouldn't talk about it either," he said.

Later on, as we wrapped up our work in the barn, one of my cousins and I started hounding Eli again, trying to find out what was wrong. He wasn't the sort of guy to act down in the dumps like that, and he really had me curious about it.

But we couldn't get anything out of him.

"If you guys knew what I know," he said, "you wouldn't talk about it either."

After we finished working, he went home and I went in to find Sam.

"Something's wrong with Eli Miller," I told him. "I don't know what it is, but something's on his mind. Something important."

"Oh, you should probably just let him go," Sam said.

I stared hard at Sam, then I shrugged.

"Okay," I said. "I'll leave him alone."

But soon I would find out what was bothering Eli Miller, and it was just another step down into the darkness of Bergholz.

11

TAKE IT OUT AND BURN IT

Later that night I sat out in the barn with my brother Edward, my cousin Melvin, and another one of the boys. I can't remember who that fourth person was. We just hung out, shooting the breeze, talking about work and wishing things could be a little different. Sam came out and joined us around ten o'clock, and the five of us talked about life. It was fun. In those kinds of moments, Sam was a great guy.

Out of nowhere, Eli Miller came out to the barn and started ranting and raving unlike anyone I'd ever heard before. He was screaming at Sam.

"I know my wife and I had problems in our marriage," he said, "but I honestly trusted that you could help us. We haven't been together for almost three years, and I trusted you with my wife. I trusted you could help us and help get our marriage back on track."

My friends and I just sat there, our eyes wide open. It was an awkward situation, being there when someone was giving Sam such a hard time. Every so often we looked at each other with surprised looks on our faces. But that was nothing compared to how we looked when Eli shouted the next sentence. He accused Sam of getting his wife pregnant.

Eli and his wife were both in their early thirties, and Sam was probably in his late sixties. It just seemed unbelievable.

I was stunned. Eli went on and on, probably for thirty minutes at least. Sam didn't say much. He just sat there and took it.

"You're a bishop! You're sixty-seven years old! You're supposed to be the leader of this community, and this is how you lead? You have got to be kidding me."

Silence fell on the barn, and we all sat there, waiting to see what would happen next. Eli stared at Sam, anger all over his face. Sam stared at the floor. We boys kept looking back and forth at each other.

Eli left as abruptly as he had entered, leaving us there with Sam. The barn door slammed behind Eli, and the silence he left behind was suffocating.

"Well," Sam said quietly. "Now I guess you know what his problem is. I guess you know why Eli hasn't been talking."

"Yeah, I guess I do," I said.

Sam looked up at me.

"Are you surprised?" he asked me.

"Kind of," I said, shrugging. "But it did cross my mind."

Sam nodded quietly.

"Okay," he said.

The first I heard any talk about cutting the beards of Amish people outside of Bergholz was on that Labor Day, at a little gathering we had at Marty Miller's house. The whole community got together, and it was a fun time. I still lived in Sam's apartment. Every family set up their own table, and I had the grill fired up and made hamburgers for everyone. It was a good day, an end-of-summer day. On days like that, I could almost believe Bergholz would turn around. Things would get better. More families would join us. Life would be good again.

By then everyone suspected Eli's wife was pregnant with Sam's baby, and people were shocked. Yet no one said anything. No one really kicked up against him. Most of Bergholz backed off from Sam even more. You'd think someone in that community would have stood up and said it wasn't right, but no one did. We all just made way for him.

There were about fifteen boys my age, between the ages of fourteen and twenty years, so we set up the volleyball net and had a game going most of the afternoon. I think it was around seven that most people packed up and went home.

I am shown here (middle of the front row) with some of my cousins and an uncle. This picture was taken between Sam's house and barn.

I spent some time cleaning up, and then Sam and I walked home together.

"I was talking to the Miller boys again," he said, "giving them a hard time about cutting their mom's and dad's hair off."

"Really?" I asked, surprised.

"Yeah," he said, chuckling to himself. "I think they might even do it."

I went back to my apartment and got ready for bed. I had to work the next day. To be honest, I didn't think too much more about it.

The next evening the Miller family pulled into Sam's place in a van. It was late. Their driver didn't get out when they came inside.

"We're going to cut my parents' hair," one of the adults said, and I couldn't believe it. Eli Miller was right there with them. His wife was pregnant with Sam's baby, and yet he was listening to Sam and going to his parents' house to cut their hair. It just seemed too unbelievable.

They asked for the clippers and a good pair of scissors. I was the only person in Bergholz who had clippers, so I gave those to them. They took them and left. I was laughing about it the whole time and shaking my head. I honestly didn't think they'd have the nerve to go through with it.

Ten people climbed into the van, all of them my mother's cousins or their spouses. Marty and Barb Miller, the parents they were going to visit, lived about sixty-five miles from Sam's place. It was September, and we were starting to harvest the fields, getting ready for winter.

The group got back that night well after midnight, and I was sitting up with Sam, hanging out in his house. I was just about ready to head to bed back in my apartment when the van pulled in and they all got out. The ten of them came walking into Sam's house, and they all seemed a little freaked out, as if they had gone a little further than even they had expected.

One of them held a large black garbage bag.

They told us their story.

One of them knocked on the door, and their mother answered in her nightgown. She let them in. The men went upstairs wearing headlamps and surrounded their father in his bed. The lights flashed in his eyes. They dragged him downstairs and cut his hair and his beard, and while they did it they made a remark about how their parents weren't Christians. Their mother was weeping, but they said they just laughed and made fun of her.

As they told the story now, everyone in the house was overexcited and loud, talking at once and interrupting each other as they shared the details of what had happened. Sam sat there laughing, rocking back and forth on his chair and slapping his knee with each new part of the story. Sam's two daughters who also lived in the house were still awake too, and they had come downstairs to listen.

After the Millers told their story, they gave me back the clippers and scissors, and they left the garbage bag on the dining room floor. That freaked me out a little bit.

"Holy cow, Sam," I said, motioning toward the black bag after everyone had left. "What are we going to do with this?"

"I don't know," he said. "Take it out back and burn it, I guess."

I lifted the bag and could tell there was something in it. I picked it up, took it outside, and started a little fire. Then I dumped whatever was in the bag onto the fire. It was hair. I could smell it burning.

After that evening, I didn't hear too much more talk about the hair and beard cutting, except every so often at the meetings we had on Friday and Sunday evenings. It seemed it would be a one-time event. It seemed crazy that it had even happened once, and I couldn't imagine anyone else going ahead with something like that. But the fact that the group hadn't gotten into trouble, combined with the thrill of the night and the stories that got passed around, had some folks in Bergholz wondering if there weren't other people they could get some revenge on.

A couple of weeks later, Sam seemed to have someone else in mind. Levi Miller, the same guy who had been in charge of the Bad Guys in the barn until they turned on him, had a brother-in-law who was concerned about the stuff going on in Bergholz. When Levi wouldn't return his brother-in-law's calls, his brother-in-law called the sheriff and asked him to go to Bergholz to make sure everything was okay. This brother-in-law's name was Davy Wengerd.

An idea arose to call Davy Wengerd and invite him to visit Bergholz. Once there, his beard was to be cut as a way of telling him to mind his own business.

This struck Sam as being particularly funny, and he laughed and laughed just thinking about it. I guess Levi thought it was a good idea too. He seemed annoyed with how often his brother-in-law was calling, and I think he was hoping for a way to get him off his back.

Levi called Davy. There were about a dozen guys crowded around the phone when he did. They decided on an evening to get together.

When Davy came down to Levi's house, some of the men slipped a laxative in his coffee, just for the fun of it, I guess. Levi and Davy ate dinner together and were sipping their coffee when Levi made the suggestion.

"We should go for a walk," he said.

"Sure, let's go," Davy replied.

They walked across the fields: Levi Miller, Eli Miller, two of Emanuel's boys, and Davy. They talked all the way. Eli Miller had the camera, and he pulled it out and took a picture of Davy.

A before picture.

"What's going on?" Davy asked.

The four men walked up to him, and one of them took his hat off.

"You're going to get your hair cut," Levi said. "And then you're going to get your beard cut."

They cut his hair and his beard with scissors, chopped it right off. They sent him on his way, but not before taking a couple of pictures. Davy fled Bergholz, and the rest of the men came over to Sam's house. I remember that the events left Levi bouncing around and laughing, as if it were the best thing he'd ever done.

"Yep, we got him," Levi said when he walked into Sam's. The whole place erupted in cheers.

12

WHAT I HEARD THAT NIGHT

Davy was the second one. I kind of laughed along through it all, because I knew Davy was sticking his nose into our business there in Bergholz by calling the sheriff and causing Levi some trouble.

"I bet he'll leave us alone now," Levi said, and I think that's how everyone justified what had happened. It was us against the rest of the world. There wasn't a whole lot of thought about whether we would get into trouble for cutting beards—at least not then, not in the beginning. After all, it was just a prank, right? That night some of the men started talking about other guys they wanted to get. It was starting to gain some momentum.

Sam and the rest of the guys started listing off some of the bishops they wanted to get, especially the ones who had reversed Sam's shunning of the people who had left Bergholz. All the men were plotting and planning, right up until the Mount Hope horse auction in October.

Johnny Mullet came up to my apartment the evening before the auction.

"I just got finished talking with Sam," Johnny said, "and we're going to go cut this guy's hair. Raymond Hershberger. He's one of the bishops on the committee, and we're going to get him. We're also going to stop at Myron Miller's place in Carrollton on the way back, and we'll get him too."

I was starting to get a little nervous about the whole thing. Who was to say the police wouldn't get involved? Who was to say we wouldn't get into trouble?

"I don't think I want to get involved, Johnny," I told him.

"No, no, no," he said. "We aren't going to let any of you guys help anyway, because you're living on Sam's place here. If you do any of the cutting, they might be able to get at Sam. We have to use guys outside of Sam's circle, to protect him."

I gave Johnny the clippers and told him where the scissors were located, the scissors I used to cut horse hair. They were very sharp. He took those, and he wasn't gone more than five minutes before Sam came up to the apartment.

"Johnny was just up at the house," Sam said, "and he's got the address for Raymond Hershberger's place. He's going to cut his hair."

"Yeah," I said. "He was out here already and he told us about it."

"By the way," Sam said, "if you stop there at Raymond Hershberger's place, you might as well tell Johnny to go ahead and cut Andy's hair too. His son. He's the guy who stole our water bucket at the horse auction one time. Might as well cut off his hair too, the ignorant bastard."

We spent the next afternoon at the horse auction, and soon it was time to leave. Instead of hiring drivers for a bunch of different vehicles to take all of us to the horse auction, we often hired a driver with a horse trailer. Four or five guys would sit in the cab of the truck, and then the rest of us would sit on chairs in the horse trailer with tarps tied to the sides to keep the wind out. A lot of us rode back there that day—maybe eighteen or twenty of us.

That night, as we pulled away from the horse auction in the dark and made our way to the Hershberger farm, I think a lot of the people in the trailer didn't even know what was going on. None of us in the back wanted to be along. It was getting kind of deep, kind of scary. It felt as if we were crossing a line.

"We gotta do it," Johnny Mullet kept saying. "We gotta do it."

He decided who would sit in the cab: he would ride up there with Danny Mullet, Lester Mullet, Eli Miller, and Levi Miller. The five of them would do the hair and beard cutting.

"You folks in the trailer," Johnny said, "stay in the trailer."

We nestled into our lawn chairs in the back. A few people had brought blankets, because it was cold riding back there. It was a long drive.

The driver and the others in the cab couldn't find the place at first. They drove around, and the more we drove around, the scarier it got. The tarp flapped against the side, and wind rushed in. Every once in a while there were headlights behind us, and that made me nervous. What if the police followed us? What if we all got arrested?

Finally the driver found the place and the vehicle stopped. It was silent, and there weren't any other lights around. Then I heard a couple of guys talking, walking toward the house. Then silence again.

Three or four minutes later came the craziest, creepiest scream I had ever heard. Guys came running toward the truck through the darkness, and the screams continued from the house.

"Go! Go! Go!" one of the guys shouted. The poor driver didn't know what was going on, and he pulled back onto the road, bouncing away on the uneven back road.

"This is crazy," someone muttered behind me. All of us in the trailer—our hearts were beating and our adrenaline was pumping. Every so often another car would pull out behind us. If it followed us for more than a mile, we thought we were done for.

The driver kept going until we got all the way down to Carrollton. Myron's place was near the top of a hill, and we pulled up and stopped. Everything was dark and silent again. I listened hard, trying to figure out what was going on.

Bang, bang, bang.

Bang, bang, bang.

Someone was knocking on the door. I heard a voice talking a little bit. All of a sudden, I heard some scrambling and a guy yelling pretty loudly. People came running across the yard and I heard another yell, a deep, angry one that sounded like a bull. That was Myron—he's a big, burly fellow. Later I found out he had five guys on him and somehow managed to get them off. They started running, and in the process Myron managed to grab onto Johnny Mullet's beard and rip a huge chunk of it out.

Johnny shouted something as they ran back to the truck. The five men jumped in and the driver took off again, but not quickly enough. Myron ran out into the night, right behind them, and wrote down the license plate number of the vehicle. But at that point, none of us in the trailer had any idea what had happened. We knew it was way more commotion than we had heard at the other place.

It was about twenty miles back to Sam's place. That was a long, cold drive. I wondered what had happened. I wondered if anyone would get in trouble. It seemed things were getting a little crazy.

Once we got home, my uncle Johnny Mullet came back and opened the door to let us out of the trailer. I stared at him for a second. Something didn't look right.

"What in the heck happened to your beard?" I asked him. His beard looked straggly and his face was red where some of his beard was missing.

He reached up and touched his chin tenderly.

"I think Myron got most of it," he admitted. "If I ever go again to cut someone's beard, I'm going to cut my own first so they can't get ahold of it."

Getting out of the horse trailer after the auction and some of the beard-cutting attacks.

By that time, we felt that we had gotten away with it again. The mood started to lighten, and we all found it funny.

"Maybe if you tell Sam what happened, he'll let us cut our hair short. That way no one can grab onto our beards."

We all sort of wanted haircuts at that time anyway. Maybe this was the excuse we needed.

The driver needed to go home because it was late, so he left. A lot of us hung out in Sam's house as Johnny and the rest of the guys described what had happened. They told us how scared the people were, how Myron had shouted and fought back. As usual, Sam couldn't stop laughing.

"Hey, if we get away with this," he said, "we'll keep going. We'll get some more."

Sam was enjoying himself. What we didn't know was that by the time the driver got home late that Tuesday night, the police were already parked in his driveway. They had received Myron's call and tracked the driver's license plate, and they confiscated his truck. I think the driver spent the night in prison while the police tried to sort out what had happened.

Some of our own men wouldn't be far behind.

13

THE RAID ON
BERGHOLZ

The next morning the driver didn't show up to take us to the horse auction. We couldn't reach him and he wouldn't pick up his phone, which worried me a little bit. He was a nice guy and he was very reliable. I don't think he had ever stood us up before.

Finally the driver picked up his phone, but I didn't learn much from him.

"I just can't make it," he said. "I can't do it." That's all he said.

I called him back an hour or so later to see if he could take us up to the auction on a later Friday, but he declined that as well.

"I can't. We have to give it a break."

A bunch of us still wanted to go up to the horse auction, so we hired a different driver. Nothing much happened that day at the auction, and the rest of the week was uneventful too. Until Friday afternoon.

That's when the sheriff showed up in Bergholz and arrested Johnny Mullet, Lester Mullet, Levi Miller, and Lester Miller. That group was in jail for two days before they were finally able to call Sam on Sunday evening.

Some of these calls were recorded. In these conversations Sam spoke in Pennsylvania Dutch and said whatever he wanted to say, as if no one would ever be able to understand. But at some point the police or lawyers brought in someone to translate those phone calls, and some of what was said would be used against Sam.

"If you get out of this, there will be a lot more hair flying," Sam said during one of those calls. It's hard to tell if he actually wanted to cut more hair and beards or if he was only saying that to keep the men's spirits up. In either case, it was a stupid thing to say on the phone, especially when you know you're being recorded.

It was also on these phone calls that the police learned about the camera that was used—the disposable camera that had photos on it of the attacks. Sam said something about how he would make sure someone got rid of it.

I wouldn't know too much about that camera, I guess, if it weren't for the fact that the "someone" he talked about—the person he would find to get rid of the camera—would end up being me.

Sam took the men's call from jail on Sunday night, and then early that week he went and posted bail for them. He also took Danny Mullet and Eli Miller along, since they had been involved, and those two men were booked and then also released on bail. You'd think that having men out of prison on bail would have slowed Sam down. You'd think it would have made him think twice about going out and looking for trouble.

You'd be wrong.

Sam started taunting Emanuel Shrock, trying to get him to convince his father to come down so they could cut his beard. Emanuel Shrock's parents had been one of the families that left Bergholz, and Sam still had a chip on his shoulder when it came to them.

Would you believe it? Even with all those guys having just been in jail, Emanuel wrote numerous letters to his parents promising they would be safe if they came to visit. He eventually convinced his father to come down to Bergholz for dinner. Turns out the sheriff was nervous for Emanuel's parents, so he came along and waited at the end of the road just to make sure nothing happened. The rest of us waited at Sam's house to get the news.

I think by then even Sam was having second thoughts.

"I'm a little nervous about this one," Sam said while we all sat around at his house, waiting to hear if Emanuel would cut his own father's beard.

"Yeah," I said. "This is crazy. We've got guys who have already gone to jail for this. And now somebody's doing it again?"

Sam nodded and kept thinking.

"Ah, it'll be all right," he said. To me it sounded as though he was trying to convince himself.

We waited until around ten that night, when Emanuel finally came into the barn. All the men from the community had gone to the barn to hang out, and the women were waiting in the house. When the door opened and we saw it was him, everyone got silent. He looked around the barn, and then a huge smile spread across his face.

"Well, we got him!" he said.

Everyone exploded in cheers and laughing, just because of the way Emanuel said it. He told us later that he had initially decided *not* to do it. He wasn't going to cut his own father's beard. But then they got into an argument, and Emanuel had had enough, so he held him down and cut his father's hair and beard.

All the women were still in the house, so Sam was going back and forth between the house and the barn, first listening to Emanuel's side of the story, then going inside to hear what Linda, Emanuel's wife, was saying.

"If the sheriff wouldn't have come in and warned us not to try anything, I probably wouldn't have done it," Emanuel said. "But when he came in, that just made me so mad I had to do something."

I don't know about anyone else in Bergholz, but I didn't know how sick Emanuel's father was. Six weeks later, he passed away, which was rough on the rest of the family. At one point I did hear Emanuel say he thought it was kind of funny that his father had to be buried with his beard and hair cut, which is a terrible thing to say. I hope he didn't mean it. I hope, like so many of the things we said and did during that time, that Emanuel was speaking through the haze of control and confusion Sam was so good at causing.

A few weeks later Edward, Melvin, Eli, and I were sitting up in the apartment above Sam's shop. It was an early November morning, cold, and we were waiting for our driver to arrive and take us to work. It was still dark outside, and I was trying to wake up. That's when my brother made a loud sound.

"What is it?" I asked.

He was staring at the window.

"Look out at the road," he said.

A whole line of cars came down the back road into Bergholz. We could see about a half-mile stretch of road from the window in our apartment. On that morning, the entire length of the road was lined with headlights. They came down around the curve of the hill, maybe forty-five or fifty vehicles total.

I whistled quietly in amazement and didn't take my eyes off the road.

"Here we go," I said, a sense of dread filling me.

I guessed that they were there for Sam and Johnny and some of the other guys, but cars kept coming in and parking. More and more cars. Guys started jumping out and running toward each of the houses: FBI, police, sheriff's department. Some of them were SWAT team members carrying shields and shotguns. There was a light on in our apartment. We thought about going down to meet them, but I didn't really want to go around a corner and surprise them, not when they were armed like that. So we decided to wait in the room until they came up.

We kept watching from the window. I heard the door in the shop beneath us slam open and voices shouting.

"Come downstairs!"

"Police!"

"FBI!"

Melvin stared at me. He looked like a deer caught in the headlights.

"What are we going to do?" he asked.

"I'm not doing anything," I said. "I'm staying right here. It's dark downstairs, and I'm not going down there to get shot. If they want me, they can come up here where they can see what I'm doing."

So we stood up there and we waited. There was a window from our apartment out to the landing, but we never saw them pass that window—they ducked below it. I still don't know how anyone could have gotten up to us that quickly, but before I realized what was going on, we heard them come up the steps.

To be honest, I was scared. There was the fear of possibly being arrested, and there was also the instinctual fear that comes when you have people racing up the stairs to your apartment, carrying all kinds of weapons. My heart was racing. The door flew open.

Three guys were standing there behind those large clear shields. They had us at gunpoint.

"Put your hands up! Put your hands up!"

The four of us put our hands up.

"Step away from the gun cabinet! Step away from the gun cabinet!"

I had forgotten there was a gun cabinet right behind us. I'm sure they weren't too happy about that. Another guy rushed around behind us once we had our hands up and patted us down.

"You guys have any knives in your pockets?" he asked.

"Yeah," I said. "I've got a pocketknife."

"Drop it."

I reached slowly into my pocket and pulled out the small pocketknife. I dropped the knife, and it clattered on the floor.

The officers stayed upstairs with us and one by one we went down and they took our information: Social Security number, name, address. Once we were downstairs, I could hear them talking among themselves.

"Should we keep them here or move them to a house?"

They decided to move everyone they found to Sam's living room. We followed them into the house. Just inside the door, I saw Sam. He was sitting there with handcuffs on and shackles on his ankles. I guess they must have pulled him out of bed, because his hair was all messed up and he didn't have his shoes on. He sat across the kitchen table from a couple of FBI agents, who took turns questioning him. Then all the other agencies had their turn with him. They were there from around six to around ten in the morning.

As quickly as the officers had arrived, they were gone. They took the men who had been out of jail on bail, as well as Emanuel Shrock and Sam. It all happened so fast.

I sat there in Sam's house. I wondered what my parents thought about everything that was going on. I wondered how long those men would be gone. It was the day before Thanksgiving.

Bergholz was completely still. Completely silent.

14

HIDING THE CAMERA

The cloud of dust had barely settled behind the long line of cars before all the Bergholz Amish gathered at Sam's house. We couldn't believe what had happened. The day before we had been looking forward to Thanksgiving. We had all planned on getting together for the meal, and then we men were going to get our shotguns and muzzle loaders sighted in for hunting season.

We tried to stay calm, and we figured we would be able to get the men out on bond after a few weeks, definitely in time for Christmas.

The FBI had left us a few phone numbers of attorneys assigned to the case, so we went out to Sam's phone and made a few calls. I'm not sure which of us did the talking. It was more like a community event, with as many people crowded around the phone as possible. We asked the attorney where the men had been taken, how long they would be there, and what we needed to do next.

I didn't go to work that day. Everything felt upside down. There were four of us boys living in the apartment at that time, and we walked back to see what shape the FBI had left our place in.

They had torn it apart. It was ransacked. Between the four of us, we had twenty-five guns for hunting, and everything was laid out on the bed so they could write down the serial numbers. There was a light stand under the opening to the attic, and they had used it to crawl up in there to search. The thing is, the attic was full of loose insulation, so there was insulation everywhere. They had made a huge mess. We weren't happy about it.

"I'm going down to see what they did to the barn," I mumbled to my roommates, who were also my cousins and brother.

I went down the steps and entered the barn. Every pair of scissors, every pair of clippers, was gone. We had some large electric clippers for animals, and they had even taken those. My own personal clippers were gone. There wasn't a pair of scissors left, not even in Sam's little store, where he sold various items to members of the community. Brand-new scissors in the pack? They took every pair. We had to go to town later that day to buy scissors, just so we would have something to cut the twine for the hay.

Soon after that the men's first hearing was scheduled, and I got a phone number for one of the federal agents involved in the raid.

"What's going on?" I asked him. "Why did you take all our stuff? Even the new scissors? Those are our tools! We need them back."

"It was on the warrant," he said, and he didn't sound too concerned. "They weren't supposed to take the new scissors."

"Well, they did," I told him.

"Which clippers were used?" he asked me.

"What do you mean?"

"I'll tell you what," he said. "If you know which clippers were used to cut people's hair, and you tell me, we can make this whole process go a lot faster."

I didn't have a problem with that, and I wanted our stuff back, so I went through a short list of items and described them in detail. Much later, during one of the days in court, I was walking along in the courthouse and a man came up to me with a big paper bag. It had every scissors and clippers in it that hadn't been used in the beard cuttings.

"I'm sorry for the mess we left," he said. "We gotta do what we gotta do." He shrugged. He seemed like a decent guy, and I thanked him.

But Sam? I don't think he'll ever get over that, the way those men came into Bergholz and went wherever they pleased, took whatever they wanted to take. He was angry about that.

Even though he was in custody, Sam still seemed invincible. I don't think any of us in Bergholz thought he was in any serious danger of spending time in prison. We all figured he would get away with it, as he always did, the same way he got away with everything else.

"The Camera" (that's how we referred to it) was this almost mythical thing that had been passed around as different people got involved in the hair and beard cuttings. Many of the hair- and beard-cutting episodes were documented on The Camera. I don't know exactly who had it at what time, but when the FBI raided Bergholz, Eli Miller had it in his possession.

He was living at Emanuel Shrock's house, and he somehow managed to keep the camera hidden during his and Emanuel's arrests. When I think about how the FBI tore our apartment up, I have no idea how he was able to keep that camera out of their hands. But he did, and Emanuel's wife, Linda, ended up with it. But she had been involved in one of the beard cuttings, so she didn't want the camera in her house.

Linda was right. She would eventually be sentenced to twenty-four months for the role she played in the beard cutting of her father-in-law. She would end up serving most of her time in a Minnesota prison. It's all hard to believe.

Her oldest son, Daniel, asked what they should do with the camera.

"Should we throw it away?" he asked me.

"I don't think you should throw it away," I said. That just didn't sound like a good idea, especially if word got out that there was a camera and then they traced it to whoever had it last. Seemed to me that if that person couldn't produce the camera, he or she'd be in a lot of trouble for withholding evidence.

Eli Miller's wife, Lovina, was in on the conversation, and she asked if I wouldn't mind getting rid of it for them.

"Look, I'm not getting rid of it," I said. "But I'll hide it for you. Trust me, I can hide that thing where no one will ever find it."

"Just throw it away!" they pleaded. "Or smash it. Or burn it."

"I'm not doing it. You smash it if you want to. But with everything going on right now, if I smash that camera, I'll tell you one thing: I'm going to jail. I don't think any of us want to go down that road."

They really wanted me to destroy it.

But at that point it was me, Melvin, Edward, and David working. Most of the other men who made money had been arrested. I ran the construction crew, and every dollar we made went toward keeping Sam from losing more than he had already lost. We also used the money to feed the families whose husbands had gone to jail. There were only four of us young men working full time. The money we made was barely enough.

At one point, one of the women came up to me and asked for a little bit of cash so she could buy groceries for her kids.

"It's gone," I said, and I felt terrible. "I don't have any money left."

She felt bad for asking. I could tell.

"Don't feel bad," I said, and in my mind I was frustrated with Sam for putting all of us in this position. "Don't feel bad for asking. I know you need money to live. But I don't have anything. It's gone. At the end of this week I'll get a paycheck, and then I can help you out."

It was on the heels of all this that they were asking me to destroy the camera.

"If I throw the camera away and go to jail for it, who's going to run the construction crew?" I asked. "Who's going to keep this place going?"

I was feeling overwhelmed at that point. With Sam gone, my cousins, brother, and I bore a huge amount of responsibility for taking care of the community. I tried hard to stay out of trouble, to not be associated with the hair cuttings, because I didn't know what would happen to everyone, including my family, if I ended up behind bars.

They all stood there quietly, and we finally came to an agreement.

"Just hide it," they said.

"Give me two plastic bags," I said, and someone brought them out to me along with the camera. I put the camera in one bag and sealed it shut. Then I put the bag with the camera inside another bag and sealed that one shut.

"I'll take care of it," I said quietly, and I left the house.

A bunch of us guys went deer hunting a day or two later. Sure, we hunted because we enjoyed it, but in those days the community needed the meat, too. If we could all get a deer, that would be a big contribution to our food supply.

I stuffed the camera, wrapped in the plastic bags, inside my pocket. I was out there with Edward, my cousins David, Melvin, and Eli, my uncle Crist, my uncle Johnny Yoder, and maybe another guy or two. There were at least seven of us, and a few of the guys knew I had the camera with me.

We eventually spread out to do our hunting, and I took a few of the trails by myself. No one else knew those trails, at least not as well as I did, so I found a tree I thought I could remember. I didn't tell anyone what I was doing. I was all by myself. I dug a hole right beside this one big tree with a stick, put the bag with the camera in the ground, and covered it with dirt and sticks and leaves.

I carved an X on the tree and quickly walked away.

I didn't want anyone else to know where it was. I figured if they didn't know, they couldn't get in trouble for not saying where it was. If they didn't know, they couldn't lie about it. I kept it all to myself. I didn't tell anyone else what I had done.

It was early morning when I buried it, and by midafternoon we had reassembled as a group. I can't remember if the hunting was good that day or not.

"Do you still have the camera?" one of them asked me, one of them who knew I had brought it with me.

"Maybe," I whispered. "Maybe not."

"What are you going to do with it?"

"You're better off not knowing," I hissed, not wanting the others to hear what we were talking about. "In fact, you don't even know I had it. This conversation never took place. Don't worry about it."

I didn't tell anyone about it, not even the cousins I was closest to.

But there's one thing I should have done differently. I thought I hid it somewhere that would be easy to find. I didn't really take into consideration how big that forest was, or how the trails seem to circle back on each other.

You can get confused in a forest like that. It can be difficult to retrace your steps.

PART III
Leaving Bergholz

15

THE *X*
ON THE TREE

"**D**id anyone mention having a camera at that time?" the prosecuting attorney asked me. My time on the witness stand was dragging on. I was only an hour or two into it, but it felt as though days had passed. It was exhausting, thinking back through those details with so much on the line.

"Yes."

"And what was said about that?"

"They said that they took pictures of him, at first he was trying to shy away from the camera, but then the last couple pictures, he didn't even shy away."

"And again, what was your understanding of why pictures were taken of Melvin Shrock?"

"Because they wanted to know what he looked like," I told her.

"All right. At some point after the defendants in this case were charged with federal crimes, did someone ask you to do something with that camera?"

"Yes. Daniel Shrock gave me the camera, said he wanted me to do something with it; either hide or get rid of it."

"And he said either hide it or get rid of it?" she repeated.

"Yes."

"And what was your understanding of why he came to you with the camera?"

That was a good question, one I hadn't considered before. Why me? Did the Bergholz community somehow see me as being linked with Sam because I lived in the apartment over his shop? Did they expect me to "take care of things" because my cousins and I were working and providing for them?

"I really don't know why he—" I began, but I was quickly interrupted.

"Objection."

The judge stared at me.

"Well, did he tell you why?"

"No," I said.

"Okay," the judge concluded. "Then, sustained."

"All right," the prosecution regrouped. "So the . . . what exactly did he say to you?"

"He came out and gave me the camera, said he wanted me to either hide it or get rid of it because he didn't want anybody to find it in their home."

"Did you ask him any questions about that?"

"No."

"All right. Did you actually take possession of the camera?"

"Yes," I answered.

"Did he actually have it with him when he talked to you about this?"

I nodded.

"Yes."

"All right. So what did you do with the camera after you took possession of it from Daniel Shrock?"

"Wednesday morning, I took it along deer hunting, and I carved an X in a tree in the woods and put it in two plastic bags and laid it down beside a tree and covered it with leaves."

"And did you do anything else after you covered it with leaves? Did you—sorry, I'm—did you do something to mark it so that you could find it later?"

"Yes."

"Okay, and at some point, did you actually provide that camera to the FBI?"

Such a simple question, requiring a simple answer. But when I had gone back out to find that camera, it had been anything but simple.

16

FINDING THE CAMERA

During the months after the arrests, things in Bergholz were hectic. We had to work hard to make sure everyone had what they needed to get through the winter. My cousins, my brother Edward, and I took care of Sam's house and farm in his absence. The weekly meetings of church-aged folks became serious as we all tried to decide what to do next. Not that we were having church or reading the Bible—those activities still didn't take place. These meetings were purely organizational.

Who was to blame for what was going on?

Who was in charge while Sam was away?

What would happen to Bergholz if Sam was pro-nounced guilty?

Those community meetings ranged from shouting matches to ones in which hardly anyone said a word. One day it would seem as if the whole thing was going to fall apart, and the next day we would feel more tightly knit than ever before.

Then came the grand jury hearings, when the courts would decide if any of the people arrested would go to trial. I was subpoenaed to testify, so I got an attorney and he walked me through the process.

"Word has spread that you were the last person to have the camera," he said, looking at me with a very serious expression on his face. "You have a choice. You can hand over the camera, an important piece of evidence in the case against your grandfather. Or you can hang on to it and probably go to jail."

That was a tough conversation to have, because in those moments I realized I was going to have to testify for the prosecution, and much of what I said would be used against Sam, and against my uncles and aunts. I wasn't happy about it, but I also didn't want to lie to cover up what they had done and then go to jail myself.

On the day before I had to go to court, I decided to find the camera and take it with me. I would give it to my attorney and let him use it as he saw fit. He thought that if I brought in the camera willingly, he could perhaps arrange a level of immunity for me in the trial. In other words, if I gave them the camera, they wouldn't prosecute me for any involvement.

That afternoon I headed into the woods, walking at a brisk pace. I was already feeling nervous about the upcoming hearing. If you spend any time with Amish folks, you know that we shy away from anything public. Most Amish people are content to live their own lives in peace, keeping to themselves and staying out of non-Amish people's business. Not only that, but being in the spotlight is frowned upon. I wasn't looking forward to heading to the city of Cleveland, sitting as a witness, and testifying against people from my own community.

Anyway, there I was, wandering through the woods, on my way to dig up the camera, and thinking a lot about the upcoming trial. I'm not sure when the realization hit me. It probably came on me slowly as I meandered along the paths. I retraced my steps. I started circling around, walking the same paths over and over. I kept going back to the same places.

But no matter where I went or what I did, I couldn't find the tree where I had left the camera.

I started walking faster. I jogged here and there, trying different paths and different hills. I was getting scared. It was getting dark. I was so frustrated, and I sat down with my back against a tree, staring down toward the road. *Why did I do this?* I thought to myself. *What was I thinking? Why didn't I put the camera in my dresser drawer? Why did I have to go and hide the thing in the woods where I might never find it?*

It was a mistake that could end with me behind bars. They knew there was a camera. They knew I was the last person in possession of it. If I didn't bring it in, they'd assume I was hiding evidence.

I went back to the first place I had checked and started making circles through the woods, larger and larger rings. Darkness fell. The woods were nothing but shadows. I decided to make one last circle. If I didn't see the X on the tree, I'd go back to the house, get a flashlight, and ask some of my cousins if they'd help me look.

Making my last circle, I saw the X on the tree. I dropped to my knees and started digging. I felt the plastic bag before I saw it. I unearthed the bag and made sure the camera was still inside. Then I sat with my back against that tree and caught my breath. I was shaking. I sat there for a little while until it got completely dark. As I started walking back toward the house, I took a couple of deep breaths. I could see the stars in the sky, way up above Bergholz.

The next day I took the camera into the grand jury hearing, and my attorney worked out an immunity deal with the prosecution. Nothing I said could implicate me in any way. I testified at the grand jury, a testimony that involved handing over the camera to the government.

The indictment was handed down just before Christmas. Those weeks are a blur in my memory, as if they never really happened, or happened in a dream.

It was quiet back in Bergholz when we got the news that Sam and others from our community would stand trial for the beard cuttings. They would remain in prison until their jury trial, something that wouldn't happen until about eight months later. We still didn't believe they'd actually have to spend much time in prison. I'm not sure why. Maybe it was our Amish mind-set—we rarely have run-ins with the law. Maybe it was a carryover from Sam's feeling of invincibility. Maybe we still didn't see why cutting beards was such a serious legal issue. Who knows.

In the meantime, as we were awaiting the trial, a few things happened in Bergholz that were important. Sam landed a multimillion-dollar contract with some gas and oil companies. They wanted to lease his land, and the money he got from that came in just when he needed it in order to pay for his defense. This had a big impact on not just the trial but also the pressure everyone felt in Bergholz. Now there was plenty of money to pay the bills and buy necessities.

Another thing that happened was that I started getting more and more into horses, buying and selling them at the local auction. My love of horses, which had begun with my first pony when I was a kid, turned into a real skill. I had an eye for horses and a natural ability to train them. Soon I was making real money by buying untrained horses, training them, and then reselling them a few months later.

Also, I began dating a girl there in Bergholz. I liked her a lot, and things got serious pretty fast. I considered buying some land from Sam, for a place where she and I could start a life.

But that spring and summer everything in Bergholz seemed to go into a holding pattern. I mean, I kept working the construction crews and, along with my brother Edward and my cousins, keeping Sam's farm together. But it was as if we were all holding our breath, waiting to see if any of the community members who had been arrested would have to serve prison sentences. The summer plodded by.

The trial started at the end of August 2012, and it lasted about three weeks. I was waiting to get called in to testify. Because I was a potential witness, I wasn't allowed in the actual courtroom until I testified. Since I was one of the last to testify, I didn't see much of the trial.

When I finally was called, it went just about the way I've written in earlier pages of this book. Those passages are taken directly from the court transcripts. Day after day, question after question, with objections and sidebars. All of it—*all* of it—was happening under the constant, watchful eye of my grandfather Samuel Mullet.

The jury thought about the sentence for five days, and during that time most of us were back in Bergholz, waiting. I guess a few folks might have gone up to hear the verdict.

I can't remember. Personally? I didn't know what to think. Was cutting someone's beard and hair worth a prison sentence? Maybe not if you put it that simply. But there wasn't anything simple about it, and it was more than that, somehow. There was the humiliation. And the revenge.

Besides, the things Sam was doing in Bergholz weren't right. I knew he wasn't on trial for those things, but in my mind it was all combined, all swirling together. I thought someone like him, someone who did those kinds of things, well, it seemed someone like that should have to pay, one way or another.

The verdict came in. The defendants—many of them my aunts and uncles, along with my grandfather—were all found guilty, on a total of eighty-seven counts. After that came the long wait to find out what their sentence would be. That would come almost five months later, in February.

Everyone in Bergholz still hoped for a miracle. No matter what Sam had done, no matter the chaos he had caused or the immorality he had been part of, most everyone still wanted our bishop back. It's hard to comprehend that. It's hard to believe people can become so dependent on a man that they'll want him back even after he does terrible things.

So we waited for the sentencing.

17

KICKED OUT

I wasn't sure what to expect when I got back to Bergholz after the trial. I had played a key role in the prosecution's case, handing over the camera during the grand jury hearings and then testifying about each of the beard cuttings. It would have seemed natural if the families of the defendants had taken their anger out on me. But you don't know the people at Bergholz.

We were family. We were tight. And when I first got back after the trial, I was mostly welcomed back with open arms. I continued living in my apartment above Sam's shop. I helped my aunts at Sam's farm, and they didn't show any signs that they were upset with me. I worked side by side with men from the community, and they never gave me a hard time about my testimony.

But I guess Sam had a change of heart about me. And he was still running things, even from inside the prison.

One evening, shortly after the trial and the guilty verdict, two of my aunts and one of my second cousins came out to talk to me when I got home from work. We were standing in the shop under my apartment.

"We've got something to tell you," one of them said, and they all looked nervous, as if they didn't want to have to tell me what they were about to tell me.

"Okay?" I said.

"You might want to sit down," they said.

"Why? Is it that bad? What happened?"

I looked around and grabbed a chair. I thought maybe someone in my family had died.

"Okay," I said again. "What's going on?"

One of my aunts took a deep, nervous breath and sighed.

"We took all your stuff and moved it back into your parents' place."

I stared at them for a moment. I couldn't really believe it at first.

"You did what?" I finally managed to say.

"Yeah," she said, nodding. "We moved you out."

I felt the rage boiling up inside of me, but I kept a lid on it.

"I'm going to tell you one thing," I said, gritting my teeth. "You are some very smart people."

"Why?" she asked me.

"Because I have a serious girlfriend. If it wasn't for her, you know what I'd be doing, don't you? I'd be out of Bergholz so fast you wouldn't know what happened."

"That's why we did it now," she admitted. "We know you won't leave while you're still dating her."

That was on a Wednesday evening, and I went back to my parents' house. Sure enough, all my things were there. It was clear to me that Sam was calling these shots from prison, and I couldn't believe that he would do this to me. I had to believe the whole thing had something to do with my testimony and the guilty verdict.

On Sunday I went to see my girlfriend. I was looking forward to getting out there and spending some time with her, especially after getting kicked out of my apartment, but she came out of the house before I had even unhitched my horse.

"I think we should talk," she said. I didn't like the sound of that.

"About what?" I asked.

"With everything going on, you know, with Sam not wanting you there on his place, well, I think we should take a break for a little while."

I was shocked.

"Why? Is it something I did?"

"No, no, it's nothing you did," she told me. "But some others told me some stuff."

"I don't even know what you're talking about," I said.

"We just need to take a break."

"Can we talk about this?" I asked. "Can you tell me what's going on?"

She shook her head.

"No, I don't want to talk about it."

She turned and walked back inside. I stood there, stunned. Reeling. My life in Bergholz was falling apart. First, I lost my place. Next, my girlfriend broke up with me. I got back in my buggy and drove back to my parents' place.

After I got kicked off Sam's place, I had to take all my horses to my dad's property. But his barn wasn't nearly big enough to keep all the horses we both had, so we rearranged the barn and made some improvements. It still wasn't a great setup, so I talked to my dad and he agreed to put an addition on the barn. He spent almost $10,000 on that addition so I could keep my horses. I think he was happy to have me home again and wanted to make it work, for my sake.

Things in Bergholz just kind of went ahead on autopilot as we waited for the sentencing of Sam and the others. Everyone had to work a little bit harder; everyone had to pitch in and do what they could. Bergholz felt quiet in those days, as if everyone were holding their breath, waiting.

My girlfriend and I went a month without seeing each other. At about that time, Ferdinand Miller and my aunt Lizzie got married. When my girlfriend and I had been together, Ferdinand and Lizzie had said we would be their best man and maid of honor at their wedding. But we weren't together anymore, so that wasn't going to happen. Besides, in our Amish community the bishop performed all the weddings, and our bishop was in prison, so there was still the question of how they would get married and who would marry them.

Lizzie still wanted Sam, her father, to marry them, so she and Ferdinand got married at the prison. Four or five people from Bergholz went along, and Sam performed the ceremony over a telephone through the glass in the visitation area. Everyone in Bergholz had been looking forward to a nice wedding—we didn't have too many weddings in those days—but they went and got married in prison. It was a huge disappointment. Everything in Bergholz felt dark. Nothing was going right.

The night of Lizzie and Ferdinand's wedding I went to my girlfriend, the one who had said she needed to take a break, and I told her I needed to know where she stood. I was tired of waiting around Bergholz if I didn't have a future there. We talked for a long time.

"It wasn't because of you that I wanted to take a break," she said. "It was because of everyone else."

I stared at her, trying to figure her out.

"Listen, we're both old enough to make up our own minds," I said. "I know what I want. What do you want? It's either a yes or a no."

We stood there in silence for a moment before she spoke again.

"Yes," she said. "I want to see you again."

So we got together again, and we saw each other just about every weekend. I got more serious about buying a piece of land from Sam. I felt I had everything lined up, so I asked her to marry me, and she said yes. For a brief moment, it felt as if life might return to normal, as if I maybe did actually have a future in Bergholz.

I started to imagine a day when Sam and the others were out of prison, when we might even start up church again. I pictured other families moving there again, and I could just about envision Bergholz as a growing, thriving place. But I was really just kidding myself. I was grasping at straws. There was no way Bergholz was going to turn around. Life as we had known it there in the early days—life as we had always hoped it to be—was over.

When Sam had been there in Bergholz, he had become fairly lenient with us young men. He realized there weren't many girls in the community, and we didn't have a youth group, so he let us get away with stuff to kind of make up for that. For example, we had an old buggy with a long antenna and lights, just for fun. Most kids in most Amish communities probably wouldn't be allowed to have something like that, and the women in Bergholz didn't like it. When Sam was still in the community, they complained to him, but he basically told them to relax.

"If you take all this stuff away from the boys, they're going to leave," he said on more than one occasion.

But after he was in jail, the same women complained about the same old things he had previously said were okay. This time, though, he gave in and told them they could tell us to stop. So the tension in Bergholz got worse. Now it was the aunts against the nephews. A few of the other folks still held grudges against each other because of the things that had happened the previous winters. On top of it all, our bishop, Sam, was in prison, waiting for his sentence, along with fifteen others. It didn't seem it could hold together much longer.

Maybe if Sam got away with a light sentence, something that involved only probation, he could come back and everything would get back to normal. Maybe the others would get probation, too, and all the children who had been moved to other families' farms could move home.

The sentencing was handed down on Friday, February 8, 2013. I was there, and I saw it with my own eyes. The judge looked down at Sam and delivered the news.

"I think a sentence of life in prison is longer than necessary and is disproportionate for what you did, so I'm going to impose a sentence of fifteen years."

Fifteen years in prison for cutting beards. I could hardly believe it. The judge then went down through the other defendants.

Johnny Mullet, Levi Miller, Eli Miller, and Lester Mullet all got seven years. Emanuel Shrock, Daniel (Danny) Mullet, and Lester Miller got five years. Linda Shrock and Raymond Miller got two years. And Lovina Miller, Anna Miller, Emma Miller, Elizabeth Miller, Kathryn Miller, and Freeman Burkholder got one year.

Nearly every family in Bergholz was affected in some way. Some kids would be without their moms (or both parents) for an entire year. Other households would have to figure out how to get by with their sole breadwinner in prison for two years, five years, even seven years.

Our community was devastated.

Within a day or two of the sentencing, I went over to talk to my fiancée. I wanted to make some solid plans. It seemed, with the sentences now handed down, we could make some decisions. I had no idea that she had already made up her mind about me.

"It's over," she said without a warning, and I could tell by the way she said it that there was no doubt. I wondered if she had been strong-armed into it by her friends again. Or maybe it was her parents. Or maybe it was just this sense that my testimony and the fact that I had provided the camera had done a lot of damage to the defendants' case.

I don't know, but it was over. I didn't even care why anymore. The only future I had in Bergholz vanished with those two words. *It's over.*

Nothing anyone had ever done to me in Bergholz made me as angry as that did. When she told me it was over, I was furious at Sam and everyone else who had been talking about me behind my back. I was so mad I was shaking. This wasn't just about a girlfriend or doing certain things. This was about my life, and it felt as if they were doing the best they could to ruin it.

"That's fine," I told her. "That's fine. But if this is it, then this is it. I'm not coming back, and what I do from now on is none of your business."

She just nodded, turned around, and went back inside.

At that point, I knew I would leave Bergholz. It was just a matter of time.

My cousin Melvin left the community for a little while, but he struggled to make it on his own. This is the same cousin who had been dragged through the icy snow on his stomach, the same one who had told some others, when I got kicked out of Sam's apartment, that if I couldn't live at Sam's place then he wouldn't live there either. He left for a while, but he ended up moving back into Bergholz and rejoining the community.

That's the hardest thing for a young Amishman if he wants to leave. Where does he go to live? He doesn't have any credit. Where will he work? He doesn't have many connections outside the community. What friends will he have?

Once Melvin was back in Bergholz, the aunts were on his case nonstop, telling him what to do, what not to do. The first thing he did when he came back was work with me and my dad on our construction crew. (After I moved off Sam's place, I went back to working for my dad.) It was strange, because we had been such good friends when we were kids, but then those previous winters had happened and things had gotten weird between us.

So there we were one day, working together up on a cold roof. It was either late winter or early spring. The roof was metal, and it was slick. I sat on the peak, holding a rope that was tied around Melvin's waist to keep him from sliding off.

"I got this," he said, but as soon as I let go of the rope, he started sliding toward the edge of the roof. I grabbed the rope and he jolted to a stop, nearly tumbling over the side. We stared at each other, eyes wide open. He had been that close to falling. His look of shock turned into a huge grin.

On a night soon after that, when we were with the rest of the Bergholz community, Melvin retold a few of us the story of what happened at the construction site.

"I had been sitting there on that roof thinking no one in the community cared about me," Melvin said. "But then I started sliding down the roof and Johnny here, he reached over and saved me, grabbed that rope. That's when I knew."

We waited.

"Knew what?" someone asked.

"I knew someone in Bergholz cared enough to keep me from going over the edge."

Word of this story got back to Sam. His response? "Johnny and Melvin can't spend time together anymore, not if they want to stay in Bergholz."

Melvin wasn't allowed to see me or talk to me. At least that was the word from Sam. We were both out of his good graces, so he didn't want us teaming up and getting more people on our side. He split us up.

One of the ways Sam kept control of Bergholz was by keeping people guessing. One moment he said this, the next he said that. One moment this person was a Bad Guy, the next he was a Good Guy. One moment you were allowed to do something, the next moment you weren't.

I guess it shouldn't have surprised me that a week after Sam issued the order from jail that Melvin and I couldn't hang out together, he changed his mind.

"I guess they can be together," he told my aunt, and she passed the news on to Melvin and me. That's when Melvin moved into my parents' house.

After that, living and working together, Melvin and I talked a lot. We remembered what Bergholz had been like in the beginning, what a great place it had been when it was just starting out. We talked about all the people who had left during those in-between years. We wondered what had happened to some of our old friends.

That's when we started planning our exit.

18

BERGHOLZ, A CULT?

As I mentioned earlier, I started playing with horses when I was seven or eight years old. I trimmed my own pony's feet at the age of eight. As I got older, I was out there two or three times a week trimming my horse's hair, even when it was still short. Sometimes my mom gave me a hard time about being out in the barn so much, spending so much time making my horses look good. But my uncle Eli, the one who had a mental breakdown, always took my side.

"You let Johnny go," he would tell my mom when I was a boy. "He's going to turn into a real horseman one of these days. Just leave him be."

My uncle Eli was right. When I started getting my own money, I started buying horses. I'd get them at the local horse auction, make them look good, clean them up, break them really well so they would listen to an owner. Then a few months later I'd take them back to the auction and sell them.

My brother Edward and I both got into horses. We'd pay between $3,000 and $5,000 for a horse, and we'd usually make around $700 to $1,000 profit when we resold them a few months later. We were making good money, and soon we had twenty-two to twenty-five horses between Edward, my dad, and me.

But no one in Bergholz liked it.

"You guys take too much pride in your horses," my uncles muttered.

"You're spending too much money on those horses," my aunts complained.

"Yeah," I would reply. "Maybe. But I'm having fun and making money. What's the big deal?"

It was the fact that I was making money that went against their grain. They didn't think I could make that kind of money without being dishonest, but I told them I never sold a horse without telling the buyer everything I knew. I never sold a problem horse. I always told the buyer that if the

One of the horses belonging to my brother, Edward.

horse wasn't the same in two weeks, he should bring it back and I'd give him a full refund.

My brother and I started buying more and more horses. At the horse auctions, we started to get to know more Amish people from other communities. We'd exchange horse stories and hear about what was going on in their neck of the woods.

The more people we met, the more we realized something. Our view of the outside world wasn't entirely correct. These other Amish people weren't bad people.

Sam hadn't been telling us the truth.

"I don't like you guys hanging around him," my dad told my brother and me one day before we left for the horse auction. He was talking about our horse dealer.

"What's wrong with him?" I asked my dad. Our horse dealer was basically the guy who took care of all the paperwork when we bought and sold horses. Sort of like a broker.

"I know his dad and his uncles," my dad said. "They're not good guys. They're dishonest."

"I've never had any problems with him," I said. "I like him. He's never sold me a bad horse. I trust him."

But my dad's concerns got me thinking, so I brought it up with my horse dealer one day. He only laughed. He didn't seem to care what anyone at Bergholz thought of him. Then he turned the tables and starting asking me questions.

"What really is going on down there in Bergholz?" he asked me. "What are you guys gonna do?"

I shrugged.

"I don't know." And I didn't know. Things in the community weren't getting any better.

"There aren't any girls down there," he reasoned. "You don't have a future there. You're going to have to find a woman someday."

I laughed. "Yeah, that's true."

Later, I was talking with another English (non-Amish) guy we knew. He also knew a little bit about what was going on in Bergholz.

"Listen," he said. "You've got a phone, right?"

I did. I had recently purchased my own cell phone, something that I had kept quiet from most of the other folks at Bergholz because phones were not tolerated there. But I had one. "Yeah," I said.

"Get on your phone when you have a chance and do a Google search for the top ten signs of a cult. Will you do that?"

"Sure," I said.

Later, I did. What I found amazed me.

Absolute authoritarianism.

No tolerance for questions.

Unreasonable fear about the outside world.

Former followers are always wrong in leaving.

The leader is always right.

Bergholz, a cult? It sure sounded that way to me.

It was about nine o'clock the night my oldest brother and my youngest aunt's husband came to my parents' house, looking for me and my brother Edward. They walked into the kitchen where I was sitting with my mom and dad.

"Dad, Mom, Johnny," my oldest brother said. "We need to talk to you."

"Okay," I said. I knew it wasn't going to be good. We walked out into the entranceway, and I sat on a desk that was out there.

"I've been talking to Sam," my oldest brother said. "And Sam says Johnny's paying too much for his horses. He said I'm supposed to tell Johnny that he's not allowed to deal in horses anymore. He can only have two horses at the most at a time, and he has to keep them for a year, and he can't spend more than three thousand dollars for a horse."

I started to chuckle.

"Oh, really?" I said. I knew I wasn't going to listen. There was no point in getting nasty about it.

My brother looked over at my mom and dad.

"And I'm expecting you two to make sure this kid listens."

That's when I lost it.

"You can go back out the same way you came in," I said, my voice getting louder and louder. "And don't bother coming back! I'm not listening to you. If I have to live two houses down the road and leave the Amish in order to sell horses, that's what I'm going to do. I won't stop unless I decide to stop. Why should I? I'm not being dishonest. I'm not cheating anyone! All I'm doing is having fun and making a little money. You're not stopping me."

It got real quiet. My brother looked at me.

"That's just what Sam said," he said.

"Whatever," I said.

Dad followed them outside. I went back in and my mom was on the couch, crying.

"Please listen to them," she said, looking up at me.

"No," I said. "It's my life. It's my money. If I want to have ten horses and pay ten thousand dollars apiece, what are they going to do? As long as I have my own money, they can't do anything."

My dad came back inside.

"I wish you'd just try to do what Sam said."

"Dad, I'd lose money doing it that way. There's no way."

Sam found out I wasn't going to listen, and he wanted to talk to Edward and me on the phone. At that point he was making a few phone calls a day, but he only had a certain number of minutes per month. We took the call on speakerphone in his house, on his phone, which had been moved from the barn to his kitchen after the arrests. We sat there and listened for the first few minutes while he talked about the weather and gabbed about other stuff. After a little while it seemed he wasn't even going to bring up the horse-dealing stuff.

"By the way," I said, "what's all this about us not selling horses?"

"What?" he asked in an innocent voice.

"My brother came over with Ferdinand and said I can't deal horses anymore."

"Oh, I never said that," Sam said.

I told him their exact words.

"No," he said again. "I never said that."

"What am I supposed to believe?" I asked him. "What am I supposed to do?"

Sam went into a long talk. "I just don't want you guys having too many horses. Maybe four or five at a time. Make sure you keep them a couple of months. Buy fresh horses. Maybe keep your spending down to less than five thousand dollars for each horse."

I glanced over at my brother Edward.

"That's what I've always done," I said. "That's how I've always operated."

Edward and I walked away from that conversation shaking our heads.

"Someone is lying," I said. "And I'm going to find out who."

19

"I WILL NEVER SEE YOU IN THE AFTERLIFE"

Edward and I walked across the road to where Ferdinand and Lizzie lived. Ferdinand was sitting on the rocking chair, watching us walk toward him.

"It seems like we need to have a chat," I said.

"Okay," he said.

"Somebody's lying, and I want to know who it is," I demanded.

"I don't know," he said. "What's someone lying about?"

"All of this horse-dealing nonsense," I told him. "You and my brother Floyd came over and told me I can't deal horses anymore."

"Sam said so," he replied.

"Evidently he didn't," I said. "I just got off the phone with him and he told me he never said that."

"I don't know," Ferdinand said. "That's what someone told us."

"Sam says he didn't. You say he did. I don't know who to believe."

Lizzie must have heard us talking, because she came out to where I was standing.

"I guess you guys will have to decide what to do," she said.

"I'm going to deal horses because that's what I was going to do anyway, no matter what Sam said."

"He's probably just telling you what you want to hear," she said, getting a little angry.

"If he wants to lie to me, that's fine," I said. "Just because he's Grandpa doesn't mean he's always right."

"You can do whatever you want to do!" she said.

Edward and I stared at her for a moment. It was becoming hard for me to understand how everyone in that community could follow Sam so blindly.

"So you're telling me that everything Sam ever did was right?"

That's when she really flipped out.

"That's exactly what your problem is!" she shouted. "You're too worried about what Sam is doing! And that one thing he did isn't any of your business anyway!"

"I wasn't talking about Sam having a baby with his nephew's wife, but if you want to talk about that, it's up to you."

Lizzie stared at me through the silence. We had been good friends at one point in our lives. It still amazes me how one man managed to split so many people apart.

"You just go and live your life. If you have any problems, don't come crying back to me," she said.

"You don't have to worry about that," I said. "I'm fed up. I'm done. No one's telling the truth here anymore. Never did, actually. I won't be around for much longer."

Soon after that, the community made it clear that my brother Edward, my cousins Melvin and David, and I were no longer allowed to go the Bergholz meetings they had on Sunday evenings. It was basically where they talked about the issues confronting the community now that so many members were in prison: who was working, who was in charge of helping out the women at their farms. That kind of thing.

On a Sunday evening in December, the first winter after Sam and everyone else received their sentences, Edward and I hooked up our horses after everyone had gone off to the meeting. We were both fed up with everything. We put on our cowboy boots, coveralls, and hoodies, even though our community disapproved of that kind of clothing. I figured that if they wanted something to complain about, we'd give them something to complain about.

Edward and I went down to the house where Melvin and David were staying. They had a little harness shop there and had started a small fire in the barn to warm things up. The fire felt great, and we sat there in the shop for hours, just talking. The four of us had been playing around with the idea of leaving Bergholz together.

"Hey," David said, "I'll get out the radio!"

He brought out his CD player and we listened to some music that we all liked, Boxcar Willie and Conway Twitty. We were having a good old time, just hanging out quietly in the barn. At around ten, I stood up and stretched.

"I'm about ready to go home," I said, not looking forward to heading out into the cold weather. There was now a wet drizzle too, which was turning into rain. We had left our horses and sulkies (two-wheeled carts) over to the side so that when Eli, David and Melvin's brother, came home, he'd have plenty of room to get into the barn.

I looked outside and saw that he was coming down the lane.

"We should probably go," I told Edward.

But ten minutes later, the four of us were still talking. That's when Eli came storming into the barn.

"You guys aren't putting your horses in my barn," Eli said in a stern voice. I could tell he was angry at us for the way we were dressed, for the way we flouted the rules. "I put your horses up by the hitching rail. You'd better get out of here."

"As soon as we're ready to go, we'll leave," I said, sitting back down.

"This is my barn," he said again. "You should leave."

Melvin lost it.

"Excuse me," Melvin said to his brother, "but you don't even work. You sit at home and spend the money David and I make. It's not just your barn, and if my friends want to come and tie their horses in our barn, then I don't want you moving them out to the hitching rail."

Suddenly there was a fight in the barn. Eli stormed out and Melvin was fuming mad.

"It's okay, Melvin," I said. "It's not a big deal."

I went out and brought the horses back to the barn. We decided we should stay for a little while, just to see what was going to happen.

Fifteen minutes later, Eli came back in with my older brother, Floyd. They came in, and they were shouting all the way.

"This is what you do?" they asked in loud voices. "This is how you get to heaven, sitting here with cowboy boots and listening to country music?"

"I don't know," I said in a quiet voice. "But you don't have to scream. This is just a little shop. We can hear you."

They flipped out again, ranting and raving. After a lot of back and forth, my brother calmed down a little bit.

"Just go home," he said, staring at me.

"I was about to go home before you guys came in here and started a fight," I said. "If you would have waited, I'd be home by now. But now that you're here, we might as well tell you: We have plans. We're tired of this cooped-up Bergholz thing. We're going out to Gallipolis for the weekend, just to see how they do things at another Amish community."

"If you do that," my brother said, "you don't have to worry about coming back."

The four of us laughed.

"Don't you worry," I told him. "We'll be coming back. We're not going out there to stay."

They started getting upset again.

"Now you know everything," I said. "We got cowboy boots and radios, overalls and hoodies, and we're going to another community this weekend. It's not so bad, and there's nothing you can do about it."

We sat there and argued back and forth like that until one in the morning. There were long spells of quiet as we tried to outlast each other. Finally, my brother and Eli walked toward the barn door. My brother turned around before he left.

"I will never see you in the afterlife."

Those were the last words he ever said to me.

I've seen him a few times since, but he never says anything.

Melvin called me the next Tuesday night. "Where are you?" he asked.

"I just started home from the job site. What's up?"

"Some of the guys are here at my dad's house. They have a pickup and a trailer, and they're packing my stuff and David's stuff. They're moving us into your dad's place."

"They're *what*? Where in the world are you guys going to stay?"

At that time, our house held me, my dad, my mom, my brother Edward, two of my sisters and a younger brother, plus Lester Miller's children (he and his wife were in prison). There were seven kids in the house, and they were going to move two more young men in with us.

"This is totally ridiculous," I said. "Stall them for forty-five minutes."

"What am I supposed to do?"

"I don't know; just stall them," I said. "I'll be there as soon as I can."

I got home, dropped off my younger brother, and took my lunch box inside.

"Where's Dad?" I asked my mom.

"He's down at Emanuel's house, but he'll be back. Just stay here."

"No, I'm not staying here. I know what's going on."

"Please, stay here. Don't go down there making a fuss and getting mad."

"I'm sorry," I said, "but I didn't start this mess. Melvin wants me there. We're friends, and we stick together."

By the time I got down there, my dad, Marty Miller, and Allen Miller had most of the stuff loaded. They had thrown all my cousins' things in garbage bags and boxes and thrown everything into a trailer.

"What kind of crazy idea are you going to come up with next?" I asked, and all three of them looked around at me, surprised to see me there.

"Sam said we had to do it," one of them replied.

"Would you jump in the river if he told you to?"

They stared at me. The blind obedience to Sam was really getting to me by then. I couldn't understand why everyone did anything he said, even then, when he was calling the shots from inside prison.

"I bet you wouldn't buy a car if he told you to, would you?" Melvin asked them.

"No," the three mumbled.

"Then why are you doing this?"

"Because Sam said so."

That's when I dropped the bomb.

"Here's the thing," I said. "Melvin and David don't want to move to my dad's house. They're leaving Bergholz. You might as well know it. It will be just as easy for you to take their belongings down to their new place."

"Oh no, we can't do that."

"Why not?"

"Sam said we had to take their stuff to your dad's house."

"Fine," I said, shaking my head, the frustration growing. "Hank's box trailer is sitting at the house. Haul their stuff there if you want, but you're putting it into that trailer."

They agreed.

They took my cousins' things up to my dad's house and then loaded it all into Hank's trailer. Hank was a non-Amish guy we knew who was helping us with our preparations to leave Bergholz. He drove off with Melvin and David and all their earthly belongings. I took a deep breath and turned to my parents. It was time to tell them I'd be leaving, too.

20
DRIVING AWAY

I stood there with my brother Edward inside my parents' house, the dust from my cousins' moving truck still settling on the road out of Bergholz.

"If you're not going to reason with anyone," I told my mom and dad, "we can't stay. If you're just going to go around blindly doing what Sam tells you to do, there's no point in me and Edward being here."

My mom got upset. "Couldn't you try it just one more time?" she pleaded. "Please try it. Give everything up. Try to do whatever Sam tells you to do. Just give it one more chance."

I shook my head. I told them I'd bent over backward for years trying to make people there happy. I reminded them of how I had built a sulky that they didn't like and Sam didn't like, so I sold it.

"I can't continue doing this," I said, focusing on my dad. "If you can give me one solid reason, from my point of view,

that I should stay, then I'll think about it. One good reason
to stay."

My dad looked at me for a little bit. His eyes were blank.

"I can't," he finally said.

I nodded slowly. I didn't like it, but I didn't feel I had
any options.

"That's why I can't stay here," I said. "No one can give
me a good reason why I should."

My dad and I had a few more conversations that week
about Edward and I leaving.

"You know what I'm talking about, right, Dad? Look
around! Bergholz doesn't even have church anymore! We're
doing nothing but sitting around here fighting, always point-
ing the finger at the outside Amish, blaming them for everything that's gone wrong. It's obvious the problem isn't them.
It's obvious where the problem is."

I could tell my dad was thinking hard about what I
was saying.

"Well," he replied, "if that's the case, then that whole
winter, what everyone went through—having their hair and
beards cut, Eli being crazy like he was, writing all our sins
down, people staying in the chicken coop—that would have
all been for nothing."

"Not really," I pleaded with him. "You don't have to see
it that way. It doesn't have to be for nothing. If you got
something good out of it, then keep it. You don't have to
let the good go. I'm not the same as I was before everything
went crazy, and it did change me. It did make me who I am.
I don't have to let that part go."

My dad looked at me, really looked at me. For a moment
I thought I was getting through.

"You don't have to continue living like this," I said.

But the haze of Sam's leadership is strong. "I can't go out there," my dad said. "I can't leave Bergholz and try associating with my family, my brothers. I know how they live. I know what they did when they were growing up."

"And they know what you did too," I said. "How do you know they haven't changed? How do you know? Everyone changes as we get older. No matter where we live or what kind of church we go to, everyone still changes."

He nodded slowly, but I could tell he wasn't convinced. He walked back into the house.

I had a few talks with my mom too, about what life would be like after I left Bergholz. "Bergholz will get better," she said. "Just stay. You'll see."

"It's not going to be okay, Mom," I told her. "The only thing that's going to change is that more and more young people are going to leave."

She started to cry quietly.

"I always wanted to be a grandmother," she said. "If you leave, my hopes and dreams are crushed."

"Can you hear yourself?" I asked her. "You want to be a grandma, but you want me to live here in Bergholz, where there are no girls for me to marry?"

"I'm not going to give up," she said, as if she hadn't even heard me. "Someday, one day, you'll have kids and be married and come back to Bergholz."

I nodded.

"You're right, Mom. Someday I will get married. Someday I will have kids, and I'll gladly bring them back here to see their grandma and grandpa. I don't care if you're Amish or not. But I won't live here again, not as an Amishman. Not ever."

Edward and I left Bergholz three days after our cousins left. It was a Friday. The men in the community were cutting ice, and I figured that would be the last thing I could do for my dad. So I helped him haul the large blocks from the lake to the icehouse. It was quiet work.

Later on that evening, Hank came with his trailer again and took Edward's and my stuff. After that, a guy driving a stock trailer came to collect our horses, and we helped load them. After that we went back inside to say goodbye to Mom and Dad.

"If you need anything," I said, "or if anything comes up, please call this number." I handed them a piece of paper with my cell phone number on it.

My mom and my sisters were crying. My younger brother was just sitting there. He wanted to go, but he wasn't old enough to join us. We went outside, and my dad came along behind us. That's when I heard him crying. My own dad. I turned around and faced him.

"You know this isn't what we wanted," he said. "You know this isn't the way we wanted it to be."

That was the worst feeling in the world, seeing my dad cry. That was the only time he ever expressed any regret about anything that happened in Bergholz. It was also the only time I saw my dad cry. If I think about it too much now, it tears me apart.

My sister Martha also wanted to leave with us, but I told her to wait. I didn't know what we were getting into.

"If we see that it works out," I told her, "I'll come back for you."

But soon after we left, everyone had her convinced they were right and we were wrong. It's one of my greatest regrets. If I could go back to that moment in time, I'd take her along with us in a heartbeat.

So how did I feel driving away from Bergholz? It's hard to describe. I couldn't think about it too much. I tried to block out everything from my mind. I tried to focus on the horses we were taking to the auction, how much I had paid for them, how much we should get for them. But my heart was ripped in two. I knew what I wanted for my life, and if I stayed in Bergholz I wouldn't attain any of those things.

At the same time, I felt terrible about leaving my parents. They were getting older, and I know they could have used my help around the farm. I hated to think about leaving them there in that community. I hated to imagine them growing old in that darkness.

I didn't know when, or if, I would ever see them again.

21

MY NEW LIFE

I think most people stayed in Bergholz because they honestly believed that if they left, they would go to hell when they died. I believed that myself for a long time. But I finally got to the point where I realized I could never please the folks in Bergholz anyway. I could never live the kind of life they expected, because the expectations were always changing.

Sam's wife, my grandmother, died after everyone was in prison. That was a sad day. Sam made a big promise right after she passed away. He said that when everyone got out of prison, he'd start up church again. I don't know why he says these things. Maybe he's still trying to control people in one way or another, but I know his promise won't hold up. And even if it does, what difference does it make at this point? After everything that happened?

I can't help but think back on how Bergholz was when it first started, how friendly everyone was and what a good place it was. Everyone joined in on everything. We were good neighbors to each other.

But now it's just everyone pulling into their own little shell. It seems more isolated than ever. You'd think that with a community that small, all the adversity they've been through would draw them together. But from what I hear, there's still a lot of bickering and fighting.

I don't know if that will ever change.

Once I got out of Bergholz, I lived in a whole different world. I felt so much better than I did when I lived there. I got a job working construction and lived with our friend Hank and his wife. They shared their home with us and took in my cousins, and my brother, and me. We went about the business of building new lives. It wasn't easy, but it was a lot better than the stuff we lived under in Bergholz.

When I first got out, I didn't know many people, so it was a little boring from time to time. I started checking out Facebook, and it was a good way to connect with other people in the community, friends of friends, that kind of thing. I found a few folks my age who had left the Amish.

There was one name that kept popping up as someone I might know: Clara Hostetler. I looked at her page and couldn't figure out why I was supposed to know her. I got off Facebook, did some work around the house. Later that day when I got back on, there she was again: Clara Hostetler. So I sent her a friend request. I went to do some repairs on the house, thinking it might be a couple of days before I heard from her.

Well, it just so happened that she was bored that night too, and she accepted my friend request right way.

"Clara Hostetler has accepted your friend request," it said on my phone. That caught me off guard. I looked at a couple of her pictures and noticed that in some she was dressed Amish and in others she wasn't.

"Did you leave the Amish?" I messaged her.

"Yeah," she wrote. "Are you Amish?"

"Not anymore," I replied, "and I probably never will be again."

"Me, neither," she wrote.

"Who is your dad?" I asked. It's a common question among the Amish. It can help you figure out who someone is, where they're from, that sort of thing.

But she got a little defensive. "Why do you want to know?" she wrote back.

"I don't know," I wrote. "Maybe I know him."

I was out late that night. When I got home, I took a shower and cleaned up around the house. The next morning I was sitting there with Edward and my cousin when I got another message from Clara.

"Where are you from?" she asked.

I typed one word.

"Bergholz."

She couldn't believe it. Her uncle-in-law's sister lived there. She was surprised because she thought the oldest boys there weren't more than fifteen years old, certainly not old enough to leave the Amish. I guess that's another example of just how isolated we were in Bergholz.

Clara wanted to know why I had left. "If you really want to know the whole story," I wrote to her, "we should meet up. We're going to blow up our phones doing this. I'll take you out and buy you dinner."

"How do I know you don't bite? What if you're creepy?" she asked.

I had to laugh at that one.

"I only bite my food," I replied. "And as far as being creepy, I don't know you and you don't know me, so I'm taking as much of a risk as you are."

Since leaving Bergholz I had gotten my driver's license and purchased a truck. I drove it over to Clara's house, and she climbed in. It felt a little awkward at first, and everything was quiet as we drove to a little restaurant close by. I ordered a steak and told her to get whatever she wanted, that it was on me. I think she got tacos because it was the cheapest thing on the menu and she felt self-conscious about me buying her dinner.

I told her about Bergholz and why I left. That was a long conversation, and she had a lot of questions. I was honest with her; I didn't have any reason not to be. She was probably the first person I told that whole story to, and it felt good to talk about it.

"Hey, do you have your license?" I asked her.

"Just my permit," she answered. "I can't get my license because I'm too busy with work."

"Come on," I said. "You can't be any worse than my cousin. There are some back roads out here if you want to drive my truck."

"I'd like to," she said in a hesitant voice, "but I don't know if I should. I've only driven twice before. I might wreck your truck!"

"That's why I have good insurance," I said. "Let's go."

We left the restaurant and went out to my pickup truck. I showed her how to adjust the seat and the mirrors. She only knew the gas and the brake; that was it. There were a lot of big hills and curves, but she wasn't doing too bad. I might have had to give the wheel a nudge every once in a while, but she was only going twenty-five or thirty miles per hour. It wasn't exactly high-stakes stuff.

We came to a T in the road, and I told her to make a right to go down to the lake. She went to make the right-hand turn, but after she made the turn, she didn't let the wheel correct itself, and we drove straight into the ditch, right into a bunch of yellow bushes.

Clara was freaked out.

"It's okay," I said, grabbing the wheel. "Hit the gas." So she slammed on the gas and we flew backward, up out of the ditch.

We got a little farther, but the road that went back to the lake soon formed a hairpin turn. We went into the ditch again.

"Just relax," I said. I had to smile at ending up in the ditch twice. "Put it in reverse and back out nice and easy."

So she did. Eventually we made it down to the lake.

I was nervous about being with Clara at the lake. What would we talk about? At Bergholz we weren't allowed to hold hands when we dated, and I didn't know what to say at first.

But we sat at a picnic table and I turned on some music on my phone. Before long it felt easy to talk to her, and as if we'd known each other for a long time. It was an epic first date.

Clara and I have been together ever since. She is someone who accepts me just as I am. We laugh a lot together, and after all I went through at Bergholz, she gives me hope for the future.

I did see my dad again, about a year later at the Mount Hope horse auction. That was the same auction I'd gone to with my dad when I was a boy. It was the first we had seen each other since I left, and I was really happy he was there. Somewhere along the line he had gotten the nickname "Papa Smurf," and even the drivers who gave him a ride would call him that.

"How's Papa Smurf doing?" I asked as I walked up to him. He didn't make any move to hug me or shake my hand, so I just smiled at him.

He didn't say anything.

"Buy any horses yet?" I asked him.

"Nah," he said.

"Don't you need some horses?" I asked him.

"Yeah," he admitted. "I need a few horses."

I pointed at one on the block. "That one would look really good with your buggy."

He didn't say anything.

"You still have that horse I sold you?" I said, trying again. "That big bay?"

"Yep," he said.

"Do you still like him?"

He nodded. He only said what he had to say.

"Do you want to meet Clara?" I asked him.

"Just go away," he said quietly.

That made me mad. "We're adults," I said. "Can't we talk?"

"You want to talk?" he asked. "Then come home and behave yourself. Come back to Bergholz, rejoin the Amish, and then we'll talk."

"I'm not going back, Dad," I said. "You're going to be a granddad whether you want to be or not. Clara's pregnant. I just thought you might want to meet Clara, the mother of your grandchild."

"Just go away," he said again. "If you respect us, you'll stay away."

I turned around and left. It was hard, realizing that my dad still felt that way. I had hoped things could be different.

I saw my mom once, and I tried to introduce Clara to her, but she flat-out ignored me. *Once the baby is born, we'll send them pictures*, I thought to myself. *They can throw the photos away if they want to, but they'll have to look at them first.*

I don't know if they'll soften with time. Maybe they will. Give it ten years, that's what I tell myself. Give it time. I can see them maybe coming around, someday. My dad is fifty-six and my mom is fifty-one. The thing that worries me is that if something were to happen, I don't know if they'd even call me.

It hurts that they won't talk to me even a little bit. To be honest, I don't like to think about it too much.

We went into the hospital at midnight early on August 31, and all the scans showed that the baby was strong and ready to be born.

The doctor induced Clara shortly after we arrived, and then we waited. I was in and out of sleep most of the night. It was hard to believe I would be a dad. I thought a lot about my own parents, and I wondered what emotions they had experienced the day I was born. I guess it was a lot like what I was experiencing.

About a week before the baby was born, we had been at a friend's house. He had steaks on the grill and was making up a nice meal for us.

"Are you excited about the baby?" our friend had asked me.

"I'm not sure," I admitted. "I'm a little worried that the whole thing will gross me out. Seeing a baby come out like that? I don't know."

My friend smiled. "Nah," he said, confidence in his voice. "I don't think it will gross you out. I think it will be the most amazing thing you've ever experienced. You'll see."

When the time came—and it came at 11:26 that morning—I have to admit: it was amazing. Clara did a fantastic job. I got to cut the cord.

Esther Jane was born.

It's crazy to think that little Esther is mine. Ours. I don't get to spend as much time with her or Clara as I'd like. My construction hours are long, and in the evening I've been doing some horseshoeing for the Amish folks around these parts. It's something I've always enjoyed doing, and it's decent money. Now that we have Esther, a little extra money is always nice.

The day Esther was born, I came home around six in the evening to take a shower and get some clean clothes. I was also grabbing a few things to take back to the hospital for Clara. I had a few extra minutes, and I called my parents. They had recently had a phone installed on their property, in a shanty outside the house. No one picked up the phone, so I left a voicemail for them.

"Hi, Mom and Dad, this is Johnny. I just wanted to let you know we had a baby, a girl. Her name is Esther Jane. She's real pretty. You're welcome to come and see her if you'd like. Or we'll come over to your place and bring her along."

I left them my phone number again, and I hung up. I sent them a birth announcement with a picture a few weeks later.

But I never heard from them. Not once.

Some people ask me these days how I feel about God. Some people wonder, after what I went through, after being in that kind of a community, how those experiences affected my belief, my faith.

Coming out of something like that? Well, it's hard to explain. I mean, I believe in God. I believe there's a God. Probably the way most people do. What happened in Bergholz hasn't changed that.

The biggest thing that's changed is that I just don't have any interest in church. I tried going to a few different places and even found one that I liked. The people were nice. The service was good. But the desire to go to church is completely missing. It's not that I'm afraid. It's not that I'm angry. I don't know what it is. I'm not saying I shouldn't go or that church isn't important. I guess I'm just taking it a day at a time right now, trying to figure out where life is taking me.

I think that people who go through a Bergholz-type situation each respond differently. My cousin, for example: after we left, he found a church he liked within two or three months. He goes every Sunday. He really likes it. So I guess these things affect people in different ways.

Then Esther was born, and I definitely felt a subtle shift in my thinking. Her birth didn't affect the way I think about God, but I have to admit I had kind of given up on religion. After she was born, I felt motivated to find a good church. I want her to grow up in church. I want her to have a group of people she belongs to. So I think I'll come around to it again someday. I guess I just need a little time.

These are the things that happened to me. This is what life is like after leaving Bergholz. Am I happy about everything I did in those days? No, I can't say that I am. I'm certainly not proud of some of the things I was part of. I feel bad about the things Bergholz did as a community.

But everything that happened led me here: to Clara and Esther and a new life. It's just as I told my dad: You don't have to throw it out. Not even the bad stuff. You just take all of life, accept where it's led you, and move on.

I don't live with regret. Actually, I have a lot of hope these days.

I think it's going to be a good life.

THE AUTHORS

 **JOHNNY MAST** grew up in the Bergholz Amish community in southern Ohio. Mast left Bergholz several years ago and now works on a construction crew. He and Clara have one young daughter and live in Middlefield, Ohio.

 **SHAWN SMUCKER** is the author or coauthor of eight books, including *Twist of Faith* and *Think No Evil*. Smucker is a graduate of Messiah College and attends Saint James Episcopal Church. He and his wife, Maile, and their children live in Lancaster, Pennsylvania.